herbs

by Eleanore Lewis

Better Homes and Gardens® Books
Des Moines, Iowa

Better Homes and Gardens® Books
An imprint of Meredith® Books

Herbs
Writer: Eleanore Lewis
Editor and Project Manager: Kate Carter Frederick
Art Director: Lyne Neymeyer
Project Coordinator: Beth Ann Edwards
Research Coordinator: Rosemary Kautzky
Copy Chief: Terri Fredrickson
Managers, Book Production: Pam Kvitne, Marjorie J. Schenkelberg
Contributing Copy Editor: Patrick Davis
Contributing Proofreaders: Kathy Roth Eastman, Maria Duryee,
    Sharon E. McHaney
Indexer: Jana Finnegan
Electronic Production Coordinator: Paula Forest
Editorial and Design Assistants: Kaye Chabot, Mary Lee Gavin,
    Karen Schirm

Meredith® Books
Editor in Chief: James D. Blume
Design Director: Matt Strelecki
Managing Editor: Gregory H. Kayko
Executive Editor, Home Improvement and Gardening:
    Benjamin W. Allen

Director, Sales, Special Markets: Rita McMullen
Director, Sales, Premiums: Michael A. Peterson
Director, Sales, Retail: Tom Wierzbicki
Director, Book Marketing: Brad Elmitt
Director, Operations: George A. Susral
Director, Production: Douglas M. Johnston

Better Homes and Gardens® Magazine
Editor in Chief: Karol DeWulf Nickell
Executive Garden Editor: Mark Kane

Meredith Publishing Group
President, Publishing Group: Stephen M. Lacy

Meredith Corporation
Chairman and Chief Executive Officer: William T. Kerr

Chairman of the Executive Committee: E. T. Meredith III

Cover Photograph: Rick Taylor

herbs

introduction

historical perspective

For thousands of years, people have gathered herbs and used them for sustenance and healing. First, wild plants helped ensure people's survival; then cultivated plants evolved and became an indispensable part of the household due to their various practical uses.

Through the ages, as herb use has persisted and expanded, herb lore has accumulated. The plants have been used in every culture around the world for their flavors and fragrances, as well as their domestic and cosmetic uses.

Herbs continue to garner widespread favor. You probably don't strew herbs on the floor to deter insects and disguise odors as people did in medieval and Renaissance times, but you can enjoy the pleasant fragrances of potpourris and sachets in your home. Native Americans taught the colonists how to use indigenous plants and allay a wide range of maladies, from sore throats and wounds to fevers and snakebites. Although herbs are still used widely to bolster well-being, use them with care; do not construe folklore as medical advice.

inspired efforts

Herbs include an immense selection of all kinds of plants from trees and shrubs, to annuals, perennials, vines, and others for all sorts of purposes in and out of the garden. Traditional herb gardens exude old-world charm. They offer an opportunity to plant history, so to speak, in addition to still-satisfying patterns of growing herbs in gardens full of herbs only. The versatility of herbs also makes

a glance at the past

right: **Inspired by traditional herb garden designs, contemporary landscapes incorporate herbs along with hardscaping materials, such as stone and gravel, to create an easy-care setting for rest and contemplation.**

them ideal for other garden designs and landscape applications. Instead of confining herbs to an herb garden, use them to edge or mix into your perennial border. Plant them with vegetables in a kitchen garden. Group them in containers to decorate a deck, patio, or entryway. Combine them with flowering annuals for all-season color.

Whether you plant a formal or informal garden, a large area, or a city plot, you will find herbs to suit your needs, from groundcovers and climbers to shrubs and trees.

sweet smells
above left: Wreaths and similar decorations bring the textures, colors, and fragrances of herbs, such as rosemary, indoors where they're enjoyable year-round.

herbal knowledge
left: Old, beautifully illustrated herbals spotlight the medicinal properties ascribed to herbs through the ages.

selecting the best

Choosing herbs for your garden depends on how you plan to grow them and how you plan to use the plants once you harvest them. Herbs are among the easiest plants to grow. They're mostly vigorous and have few problems with pests and diseases. Although the climate of your region plays a part in determining some of your choices, you'll discover endless options, including annuals, perennials, and biennials. You'll also consider plants with tropical and subtropical origins that won't survive year-round in cold-climate gardens but thrive indoors on a sunny windowsill.

Think of herbs as multipurpose plants. Those you want to grow for flavor or fragrance also offer color, texture, and form in the garden. Visualize pungent sage with its blue flowers and grayish green leaves, picture the feathery leaves and yellow flower clusters of dill, and imagine where they would fit into your garden. Consider the harmony

choose with care

above right: Whatever purpose you want herbs to fulfill, select them carefully at the nursery or garden center. Look for young, compact plants with lush, healthy foliage and no signs of pests.

ideal partners

right: Herbs combine well with so many other plants that they provide just the right choice for a vacancy in the garden.

harvest delight

left: **When you have your own herb garden, you may harvest leaves and flowers anytime for fresh use throughout summer and into autumn. Preserve the bounty for winter use by hanging bunches of fresh-cut herbs and letting them dry in a warm, airy place.**

foliage focus

below: **Plant herbs with attention to foliage color and shape, but grow herbs for their flowers, too.**

and contrast you can achieve by combining herbs with herbs and herbs with other plants. Plan separate beds for specific uses, such as culinary or tea herbs. Above all, plant what you plan to use.

easy does it

Whether you grow herbs from seeds or cuttings or start with nursery transplants, you ensure their success if you start with fertile soil and (for most herbs) a sunny site. Herbs require little more than that. Frequent harvesting keeps plants lush and productive throughout a long growing season.

Once you've mastered the basics, learn how to multiply your herbs using various methods and you'll be rewarded with an abundance of plants. Later, experiment with different ways of preserving the leaves, flowers, and roots for future use.

herbs | 9

introduction

using the bounty

The additional pleasures of growing herbs come when you harvest them and use them for cooking, aromatic arrangements and potpourris, cosmetics, and other crafts.

The culinary applications of herbs are practically endless. Steep leaves to make refreshing or soothing teas and piquant vinegars. Blend flavorful butters and cheeses. Make gourmet pestos, spicy mustards, and sweet jellies. Combine your favorite fresh or dried herbs in blends to season and transform all your usual dishes, from meat, fish, and poultry to soups, salad dressings, and vegetables. Use herbs for grilling, baking, and even whipping up delightful desserts.

In the pages ahead, you'll see how to bring the beauty of herbs indoors and savor their colors, textures, and fragrances for months to come in a variety of herb crafts. This is when the real fun begins!

spontaneous designs

above: The decorative uses of herbs include charming bouquets, sweet nosegays, beautiful wreaths, colorful swags, herb-stuffed pillows, and fragrant potpourris. The effects will vary, depending on whether you use fresh or dried herbs.

simple pleasures

right: Herbal infusions and facial splashes are two refreshing ways to use these beneficial plants for cosmetic purposes. As part of your personal beauty regimen, herbs provide a multitude of pleasures, from invigorating or soothing baths to cleansing facials. Once you begin making your own herbal cosmetics, you'll want to share them with your friends and family.

keeping the harvest

left: When you gather herbs from the garden, you are harvesting their flavors and fragrances for enjoyment later. The endless ways to use herbs, fresh or dried, will keep you busy experimenting. During the growing season use fresh herbs as often as possible; consider how you will preserve the majority of your harvest—the air-drying method is most popular—and how you will use it. Once dried, store your herbs in glass jars until you use them in cooking or crafting. Savor them all winter.

the
gardens

the
gardens

Herbs lend themselves to so many uses that they belong in every garden. The size of your garden matters little: Most herbs grow as happily in containers as they do in the ground. Work with the space you have and design a formal or informal scheme, an entire landscape, a plot outside the kitchen door, or a handy indoor windowsill garden.

versatile plants Herbs constitute a vast group of plants, from annuals and perennials to trees and shrubs. Although most herbs need at least six hours of sun daily, many of them adapt to lightly shaded spots. Use herbs to serve a variety of your landscape needs. Surround a patio with a fragrant hedge of rosemary or santolina, for example. Edge a perennial border or path with low-growing thyme, parsley, or lady's mantle. Train a woody herb, such as rosemary or lavender, into a topiary to accent a corner of the garden. Plant tree-size herbs where they can show off through the seasons and create shade. Make a bold statement in your garden bed with architectural herbs, such as angelica, lemon verbena, bronze fennel, and costmary. Keep smaller herbs handy in a window box, an old-fashioned strawberry jar, or any attractive container. The textures and colors of herb foliage make them ideal for interplanting, particularly with roses, vegetables, and perennials. The blooms of herbs, though often subtle, add color and variety to a cutting garden.

specific uses As the following pages show, you can design herb gardens for specific uses, including decorative, crafting, culinary, and medicinal. Transform a section of your lawn into an herbal carpet. Resolve a problematic, poorly draining site by planting handsome and productive raised beds or large containers. Make a quiet sanctuary in a side yard, imitating a medieval cloistered garden. Design an adaptation of a symmetrical Elizabethan knot garden in your yard. Research the ancient medicinal applications of herbs and devote part of your garden to recreating some of that history. In a kitchen garden with a colonial-like design, grow the special ingredients for ethnic cuisine, such as Mexican or Thai. Whatever the shape and size of your herb garden, keep it close at hand to use and enjoy.

classic parterre

careful symmetry

The elements of this classic ornamental design appear simple, but the beautifully balanced symmetry of the beds and paths requires planning. Patterned after old European schemes and perpetuated in colonial gardens, parterres include neat paths and tidy bisecting beds of various geometric shapes (rectangular, square, and triangular) surrounding a central bed. A fence or hedge encloses the garden. Sketch your design ideas on graph paper or use cutouts of geometric forms, which are easy to move around.

Some of the elements adapt easily to other options: Substitute a split-rail or wrought-iron fence for the picket fence, for example. Well-constructed paths should be handsome and practical. Use inexpensive shredded bark instead of gravel, or make the paths using brick pavers, or concrete. Surround the raised beds with traditional brick instead of the landscape timber edging shown at *right*.

However, the most adaptable parts of a parterre garden, aside from its size, are the plants. Combine herbs with annuals, perennials, and small shrubs, considering their texture, shape, and color. Plant climbing roses and vines, such as clematis, next to a fence or put up trellises to support them. Edge the beds with neat herbs, such as thyme, dwarf lavender, feverfew, parsley, or catmint. If you want more flowers, include petite marigolds and mounding dianthus.

In the garden's center, place a large urn (planted or empty), a sundial, a fountain, or a treasured plant, such as a bay tree. Assign each bed a separate purpose: herbs for fragrance, cooking, or tea, for instance. Plant beds with color themes: a blue and white garden could include rosemary, borage, silver artemisia, and lavender.

structured beauty

left: This garden reflects the symmetry of a classic parterre with a central bed and matching perimeter gardens. An armillary sphere, set on a pedestal, provides the main focal point. The neat paths winding between timber-edge beds add structure to the design and make tending the garden easier.

great herbs for large gardens

angelica

artemisia

bee balm

comfrey

coneflower

costmary

fennel

hops

horehound

lady's mantle

lavender

lovage

mint

rue

sage

valerian

herb garden installation

zones	time	skill
3–10	weekend	moderate

you will need

- string, stakes, and powdered lime
- wheelbarrow
- compost, rotted manure, and gypsum
- landscape fabric
- bricks
- herb plants
- mulch: gravel, shredded bark, or cocoa bean hulls
- rake

step by step

Bricks edge the simple geometric beds and make a neat peripheral path along this pretty parterre. Gravel paths between the beds make for easy access and maintenance. The open fencing provides a sense of enclosure and privacy, as well as a perfect support for roses, raspberries, and flowering vines. The design adapts to a smaller or larger space.

formal design

right: **Four triangular beds form the basic design for this 10×15-foot herb garden.**

lay path Plot the perimeter of the **1**
garden and the bisecting paths with string
stretched between stakes. Use powdered lime
to mark the beds and paths on the soil.
Prepare the soil in the beds by amending it
with several wheelbarrows full of compost
and rotted manure. Dig or rototill to blend
these amendments with powdered lime and
gypsum. Tamp down the soil in the paths to
level them.

edge with bricks Lay heavy-duty **2**
landscape fabric on the paths to deter the
growth of weeds. Let the edges of the fabric
extend far enough into the beds to set bricks
or similar edging material on top of the cloth
and hold it in place. Set bricks end to end
around the edges of the beds. If you prefer,
stand the bricks on their narrow side.

plant Start with herbs in 3-inch to **3**
1-gallon containers. The larger the plants, the
sooner they will mature and fill the garden.
Before unpotting, arrange the plants on the
beds to determine where to plant them.
Unpot each plant and plant it in the soil at
the same level it grew in its nursery pot.
After all the herbs are planted, water the
plantings thoroughly.

mulch Spread mulch at least 2 inches **4**
deep on the paths to finish the installation.
Rake the surface to smooth and even it.
Choose coarse gravel or finer pea gravel,
shredded bark, or wood chips for
soft pathways. Cocoa bean hulls make a
chocolate-scented path but have a tendency
to blow or wash away; combine the hulls
with a heavier mulch to keep them in place.

city gardens

adapt a classic
Tuck a small garden anywhere, even in the tight space between a patio and a garage. A classic parterre works wonders with a limited area: Its formal design uses every bit of space. Simple pathways make all the beds accessible.

Both small and formal gardens require conscientious, regular trimming of plants to keep them compact and lush throughout the growing season. Use bricks, landscape timbers, or concrete blocks to outline the raised beds. Repeat the material to make paths with brick pavers, chipped bark, or poured concrete. Use fencing, trellises, or obelisks to add structure to the garden, and take advantage of the vertical growing space for tall or climbing plants, especially edible ones.

squeeze play

above: Tuck herbs into the smallest pockets of soil along a front entry, next to a walkway, or in a sunny corner. Back the plantings with a section of picket fence to add structure. Plant them in pots if you lack enough workable earth. Beware of planting edibles close to traffic flow, where they're exposed to its polluting exhaust.

suitable plants

left: Combine a parterre design with herbs, annuals, and vegetables for an all-purpose garden. Leave openings for planting areas when you lay the paths. Set containers here and there as accents. Grow creeping thyme and parsley along the bed edges. Combine compact basil and calendula with strawberries, beets, and a compact tomato plant or two in the middle of the beds. Surround the central bed with a trim hedge of rosemary or boxwood.

great herbs for small places

basil

calendula

cayenne

chives

cilantro

feverfew

germander

lady's mantle

lavender

oregano

parsley

rosemary

salad burnet

sweet woodruff

tarragon

thyme

country garden

space to spare

Large gardens are often harder to design than small ones. All that space requires judicious planning. It helps to lay out the garden in sections or themes. Make raised beds by surrounding them with brick or landscape timbers to help define the space and build well-drained planting areas. Create several small planting areas within a larger one by shaping generous islands of soil. Fill these informal gardens with plants appropriate for the site, such as a sheltered woodland glade, a rocky Mediterranean herb bed, or a border of mixed perennials and herbs.

Use fencing to add definition and eye appeal, as well as support for rambling plants, such as roses or hops. Make a large garden more attractive by including other structures. Integrate a utility shed by planting herbs and flowers around its base and training climbing plants up and over the roof. Include a bench so you may rest occasionally and admire your handiwork.

Large gardens accommodate large plants. Planting without inhibition and even allowing gregarious herbs to grow is fun—just don't let them get out of control. Plant mint, lemon balm, and oregano where you can spade out their spreading roots. Include the comfrey and variegated horseradish you've always wanted, but keep them in large pots or half-barrels.

When planning the garden, take extra precautions to outwit predators by determining how you will keep them out of your garden. The best deerproof fences stand 8 feet tall. Deter burrowing critters by extending wire fencing underground. Have a dog stand watch.

country style

left: **A two-tier garden that fits its large, sloping site brims with color and texture. In early summer, poppies, roses, and daisies mingle with herbs. All the plants have room to spread out. The shed adds a handsome backdrop. Wire fencing becomes almost invisible when nailed to split rails but helps keep out uninvited creatures, such as rabbits.**

kitchen gardens

centuries-old tradition

Kitchen gardens combine utility with beauty and grow conveniently outside the back door. If you visit historical kitchen gardens, such as those at Colonial Williamsburg and Monticello in Virginia, the traditional *potagers* in France, or estate gardens in England, you'll see neat beds containing herbs, vegetables, flowers, and fruits. The Victory Gardens of World War II were kitchen gardens, too, though not as formally laid out. They provided families with produce to eat fresh and preserve for year-round staples.

Walls, hedges, or fences protect traditional kitchen gardens from the wind. The gardens often feature a four-square design: four beds with intersecting paths that cross in the middle and a perimeter bed just inside the wall or perimeter. Take a cue from historical kitchen gardens that included a central well for a convenient source of water; instead, keep a spigot nearby.

Depending on the available space, a kitchen garden can be any size, from an entire yard to a few pots on the back steps. Include a variety of herbs, vegetables, edible flowers, and a favorite fruit tree or two, no matter the garden's size.

Large gardens provide more design opportunities. Make the layout decorative by varying the shapes of the raised beds. Interplant herbs and annuals with fruit trees and vegetables, or devote individual beds to specific plants. A mix of plants, however, provides more color and texture over a longer period. Give the garden a somewhat formal appearance by edging the beds with neatly growing plants, bricks, or sectional edgers (*as shown*).

Install a drip irrigation system to avoid dragging a hose around the site. Set a fountain or a birdbath in the center of your garden for added delight.

chef's delight

above: A kitchen garden should serve the cook. Grow plants that you couldn't cook without, such as rosemary, dill, basil, parsley, and thyme. Picked and used fresh, they turn many dishes into treats.

a living pantry

left: A small backyard is transformed into six large, rectangular raised beds linked with pathways of Mexican pavers. The space now offers an abundance of fresh vegetables, apples, and herbs. Chives, parsley, basil, and scented geraniums accent tomatoes, green beans, zucchini, and society garlic. The paths provide easy access to the 4-foot-wide beds from both sides.

kitchen gardens

companionable pairings

Long before gardeners discovered sprays and dusts, they used the still-popular technique of companion planting to protect their crops from the onslaught of pesky insects. Over time, close observation taught gardeners how particular herbs benefit other plants, especially vegetables, fruits, and roses, when planted with them. Modern research has shown that part of herbs' efficacy as pest repellants lies in the volatile compounds in their leaves and roots.

Put herbs to work as repellants by planting them under, around, or in rows between their companions. For instance, plant garlic under roses, borage along strawberries, and garlic chives between rows of lettuce and peas.

Many herbs also improve the growth, flavor, or flowering of their companions. Summer savory enhances the growth and flavor of beans. Thyme is said to bolster potatoes.

Also plant herbs, such as chervil, parsley, dill, and fennel, that attract beneficial insects to prey on the pesky ones.

all-around herbs

right: Parsley and basil, planted among a fall crop of squash, lend some protection against insect pests and contrast beautifully with a plant that tends to sprawl.

great companion herbs (and their companions)

basil (tomato)	parsley (asparagus)
chives (apple)	rue (raspberry)
garlic (rose)	sage (cabbage)
mint (cabbage)	savory (green beans)
onion (carrot)	tansy (berries)

helpful edging

far left: Edge beds with chives, garlic chives, or garlic to deter insects. Chives go well with carrots, but keep all members of the *Allium* genus away from peas and beans.

classic pairing

above left: Tomatoes and basil make a classic combination in the garden as well as in the kitchen. Basil protects tomatoes from insects. Parsley also helps tomatoes if you plant it at a distance; it attracts hornworms, which you can then pick or knock off and kill.

front and center

left: Turn your front yard into a lush garden by removing the lawn and planting a combination of herbs and vegetables. For texture, plant fennel and scented geraniums; let thyme creep between stepping-stones. Add color with pink-flower clary sage, as well as red- and green-leaf lettuces.

kitchen gardens

world travelers

Once-exotic culinary herbs from all over the world are now widely available and provide delectable ingredients in international cuisines. The plants lend themselves to delightful collections or theme gardens. Growing ethnic herbs opens the door to discovering new tastes and styles of cooking. Try herbs for Mexican, Italian, Thai, Asian, or Greek cuisine. Their flavors range from subtle, sweet, and refreshing to tangy and spicy. Many of these herbs are tender perennials that come from tropical or semitropical climates and survive winter outdoors only in Zones 9–11.

Plant a collection of international herbs in a separate bed, or intermingle a few new herbs with old favorites. Plant a global garden in a half-barrel placed near the patio or as a focal point in the center of an in-ground herb garden. Grow herbs that most of us think of as spices: coriander (the seeds of *Coriandrum sativum*; the leaves are known as cilantro), saffron (the stigmas of the saffron crocus, *Crocus sativus*), caraway, cumin, and ginger.

asian flavoring

above right: **Grow lemongrass, a tropical herb from Southeast Asia, in a pot (in all but the warmest climates) and bring it indoors over winter; it fares well outdoors year-round in Zones 9–10. During the summer months, cut its lemon-flavor leaves any time. They accent Oriental dishes, make a refreshing tea, and substitute well for real lemon flavor. Dried, steeped in water, and strained, they also make a fragrant hair rinse.**

exotic edibles

right: **Asian herbs and vegetables add interesting flavors and textures to dishes. Asian eggplant, Kaffir lime, ginger, Vietnamese coriander, and spicy Thai basil thrive in containers and jazz up a patio or deck.**

pesto perfection

left: Plant Italian herbs, such as basil, thyme, and flat-leaf parsley, in colorful cans. Poke holes in the bottom of each can for drainage. Set the plants in a place with late-afternoon shade. Water when the soil feels dry.

spicy tango

below left: Group cilantro and cayenne (or another hot pepper) in pots with a couple of tomato or tomatillo plants nearby for a handy salsa garden. Grow epazote, a classic Mexican herb that's used to flavor refried beans.

great international herbs

basil	ginger
cardamom	mustard
cayenne	oregano
cilantro	oriental chives
cumin	rosemary
flat-leaf parsley	stevia
garlic	thyme

knot gardens

design symmetry

Elizabethans made an art out of planting intricate, intersecting designs known as knot gardens. Copy a historical design or make an original one. Start by planting low hedges or creeping herbs in a simple design, such as a cross within a raised square or circular bed. For a more challenging project, design and plant intersecting circles within a square or rectangle. First, work out the pattern on graph paper; then outline it on the soil using powdered lime or stakes and string. Start with plants in 1-gallon pots and plant them a foot apart on the lines. They'll fill in within a year or two, forming short hedges or covering the ground. Select dwarf or compact plants for hedges and trim them monthly. Choose groundcovers for lower-growing designs. Contrast foliage colors and shapes to make the segments look as if they actually intertwine where they intersect.

simple shapes

above: Design and locate your knot garden to view it from all sides and above. Keep the design simple to save yourself from tedious maintenance. The intersecting hedges of santolina, framed by rosemary, need occasional trimming. Basil, thyme, and tarragon fill the triangular beds.

color contrasts

right: Mulch fills the open knots of this garden, contrasting with the lavender and rosemary plantings and keeping down weeds. Use colored gravel or cocoa bean hulls as alternatives. Substitute plants appropriate for your climate and design. Replace cold-sensitive rosemary with hardier boxwood, for instance.

attractive combinations

above: Dwarf red barberry, a compact and low-growing shrub, forms the perimeter of this intricate knot garden. Dwarf myrtle and parsley intertwine and cross within it. The myrtle (hardy to Zone 8) is pruned regularly to maintain its neat appearance. A potted gardenia tree winters indoors in all but the warmest climates.

great plants for knot gardens

boxwood	feverfew	parsley
catmint	germander	rosemary
chives	globe basil	rue
dwarf hyssop	lavender	santolina
dwarf sage	oregano	thyme

cloistered gardens

quiet sanctuaries

In medieval times, cloistered gardens were tended by monks and included medicinal and fragrant herbs, as well as plants for dyeing and seasoning. Monasteries were often the only source of medical help, though people also used many herbs as charms against various plagues. The seasoning power of herbs was also important because foods, particularly meats, quickly went bad.

Today, one of the best-known cloistered herb gardens in the United States is at The Cloisters, a branch of the Metropolitan Museum in New York City. It is modeled on gardens of the 1400s–1600s. The raised beds include historically correct herbs: chives, feverfew, hops, horseradish, lavender, lemon balm, parsley, sorrel, tansy, valerian, and winter savory.

A traditional cloistered garden is enclosed, set apart from the world but open to the sky, with pillars and walkways. In lieu of an enclosed space, make a cloistered garden in a side yard, next to an entryway, or on a balcony or a rooftop. In contemplating your version of a cloistered garden, incorporate structures, such as a fence, a trellis, or a pergola, to provide enclosure and the ambience of a medieval courtyard garden, even if you opt for more contemporary plants. Plant individual herbs in separate beds by use or grow one type of herb, such as a culinary or an aromatic variety.

pocket garden
right: **A simple planting scheme and spare furnishings create a serene cloistered garden along the foundation of a house. Graceful salad burnet dances around the feet of Saint Francis.**

hidden asset

left: This cloistered garden, only 9 feet wide, turns a narrow side yard into a culinary haven, as well as a place for meditation. The formal design features brick-edge raised beds, a brick wall, concrete floors, and ornate statuary. The concrete fountain makes water music that drowns out street noise; the lattice wall boosts the sense of privacy. Add a bench, along with a table and chairs, to provide comfortable seating and a place for quiet meals.

medicinal gardens

healthy herbs

Long before doctors and modern medicine, plants provided the most common treatments for injury and disease. Typically, gardens were living apothecaries filled with pharmaceutical plants. Although we now know that some of the old remedies are useless and even dangerous, many of today's drugs originated from herbs that have been used to treat numerous maladies over the centuries. From *Digitalis* and *Echinacea* to *Hypericum* (St. John's wort), many herbs continue to be popular and their benefits are backed by scientific research.

Peruse the contemporary reprints of 17th-century herbals, such as Gerard's and Culpepper's, which document the plant–based beliefs of folklore at the time. However, do not take the descriptions of herb use as medical advice. Also be cautious and prudent regarding modern herbalists' opinions. If, for example, you are allergic to ragweed, avoid internal use of chamomile and any other members of the *Compositae* family, which includes coneflowers, feverfew, and yarrow.

A bed of medicinal plants, however, provides a glimpse back in time to when people relied on nature for much of their nurture. Researching the past uses of herbs broadens their appeal.

nature's apothecary

right: This 40×50-foot area, situated behind a historical barn, reflects a typical colonial kitchen garden with a focus on medicinal plants. From lofty pink foxgloves (*Digitalis* sp.), colonists made a liver and spleen tonic, for example. Sweet-scented white valerian was used for sleeplessness and nervous disorders. Fennel tea helped ease indigestion.

four lovelies

above: Although these four herbs belong in any garden for their beauty alone, their possible medicinal qualities add intrigue. Purple coneflower, also known as *Echinacea*, was valued in the Middle Ages as a coagulant and used by Native Americans to heal wounds. Modern herbalists infuse yarrow to make a tea for treating colds and stimulating the appetite. According to modern herbals, the dried flowers of calendula exhibit anti-inflammatory and healing qualities when applied to wounds. Do not take it internally. Folklore describes a decoction of feverfew flowers mixed with honey for treating coughs and stuffiness due to colds; modern herbalists recommend it for migraines.

added charm

Take advantage of the ornamental uses of herbs and extend them beyond the herb garden. Weave herbs throughout your landscape where they will add diversity without adding upkeep. Use herbs to add varied colors, textures, and forms to perennial and shrub borders, and even to replace lawns.

Depend on herbs for their versatility. Many, such as sage, lavender, and rosemary, grow shrublike. Some crawl; others climb. Many herbs adapt to a variety of settings. Some thrive in both sun and partial shade; others tolerate either wet or dry conditions. Discover the beauty of herbs as hedges, edges, unusual accents, plant partners, and trees. Plant individual specimens as accents, or group plants for impact.

flowering lushness

left: A lush cottage-garden-style landscape combines herbs with shrubs, such as roses and rhododendrons, and a tapestry of perennials. Creeping herbs have begun to fill the crevices of a stone path. Lavender, lady's mantle, catmint, and santolina edge the planting area and contribute to the colorful scene.

inviting walkway

below: Herbs, annuals, and perennials enliven an entry walkway. Chartreuse-flower lady's mantle teams up with 'Johnson's Blue' cranesbill *(Geranium)* and blue salvia. An evergreen, such as an Alberta spruce tree, adds year-round interest.

herbal landscaping

season extenders
Herbs make ideal planting partners with annuals and perennials. Use herbs to form tidy edges, reach roof high as background plants, and draw attention as outstanding specimens. Some garner year-round interest. Purple coneflowers and yarrow bloom from summer through fall, for example, and add structural elements that look attractive in winter. Sage retains its silvery leaves through the winter, adding a bit of color and contrast to a stark landscape.

Throughout summer the tall stems of dill, fennel, angelica, and valerian grace the back of a border. Low-growers, such as sweet woodruff, parsley, and thyme, form perfect edging from spring through fall.

peak season
right: **Lamb's-ears, pink yarrow, borage, and pansies combine with fragrant roses to produce a pastel delight in summer.**

season-long color

left: Chives and variegated sage harmonize easily with annual bacopa and Boston lettuce. The pink flowers of roses, cranesbill *(Geranium)*, and alstroemeria appear week after week, complementing other plants and providing a long season of color.

picture perfect

left: Varying heights and foliage shapes compete for attention with the subtle colors of the flowers in early summer. Lavender, lady's mantle, and foxglove surround the birdbath. Dianthus and thyme edge the garden.

lawn alternatives

Step on a patch of ground covered with creeping thyme, chamomile, yarrow, or pennyroyal, and wonderful fragrances rise to greet you. As an alternative to turfgrass, creeping varieties of herbs make richly textured replacements for patches of lawn and are neither difficult to start nor maintain. A wide variety of low-growing herbs make delightful groundcovers, especially in hard-to-mow places.

As another option, mix herbs with cool-season turfgrasses, such as rye, bluegrasses, and fescues, to create a fragrant, blooming lawn in cold-winter regions. Sprinkle the seeds on loosened soil (where grass grows sparsely), or tuck seedlings into bare spots. Water well and keep soil moist until plants become established. Mow every other week.

curb appeal
above: In mild climates, use a sprawling form of rosemary to cover a front lawn made more interesting by shaping low berms of soil as a base for the evergreen cover.

billowing color
right: Thyme and golden marjoram, planted in colorful wedges, resemble a quilt pattern. Combine patches of creeping herbs with colored gravel for an equally graphic effect.

lying low

left: Creeping thyme and *Sedum spurium* form a dense carpet around stepping-stones. Started in spring with plants set 6 inches apart, this lawn filled in by the end of its first summer. In subsequent years, monthly shearing with grass clippers will keep it looking good.

magic carpet

left: Low-growing English thyme and mother-of-thyme, grown from thickly sown seeds, make a lush groundcover in a sunny garden. As a lawn substitute, use creeping forms of thyme which provide a dense mat as well as durability and distinctiveness.

edges and hedges

Herbs add welcome dimensions to garden designs, especially when you use them for colorful, visual interest. To play up their neat habits, plant compact, low-growing herbs as edging between beds and paths. Taller herbs, with more upright and spreading habits, make outstanding hedges that mature within a year or two and need only occasional clipping. Varieties of hedge germander (*Teucrium divaricatum* and *T.* x *lucidrys*), for instance, are taller and more upright than other common types; their leaves are glossier, too.

Combine classic hedge plants, such as lavender, rosemary, dwarf hyssop, and winter savory, with shrub roses for knock-out effects.

Edge beds and paths with herbs that reach ankle high and release their scents whenever passersby brush against them.

royal pair

above: Bushy lavender and creeping thyme demonstrate their appeal as hedging and edging plants. Both adapt well to a variety of situations.

stately hedge

right: Among the herbs traditionally used to create a hedge, lavender shines with its dense growth and beautiful blooms.

natural colors
left: Rosemary, dianthus, thyme, and boxwood perform well as edging or as hedge plants. Setting a comfortable bench among the herbs invites you to pause awhile and enjoy the sweet, pungent aromas.

great herbs for edges

artemisia	lady's mantle
basil	lavender
calendula	marjoram
chamomile	parsley
chives	santolina
cumin	sweet woodruff
germander	thyme

great herbs for hedges

artemisia	lovage
bee balm	mustard
feverfew	oregano
germander	rosemary
hyssop	rue
lavender	southernwood
lemon balm	tansy

planting crevices

Tuck small, spreading plants, such as chamomile, wooly thyme, and Corsican mint, into soil–filled pockets between bricks or stones in a path. Those herbs withstand light foot traffic.

Use other, less-durable herbs, such as creeping savory and common thyme, to fill nooks in a dry stone wall.

Start with 4-inch potted plants. Water them and then divide each one into four smaller plants. Wedge the sections into openings in a walk or in a stone wall. Add soil to cover the roots and fill the crevices. Water thoroughly.

herbal landscaping

diverse accents

Think of herbs as more than the fragrant, useful plants that you grow in a traditional herb garden. As individual representatives of a large, diverse group, they make impressive statements on their own. Architectural plants, such as angelica and mullein, demand attention. Colorful St.. John's wort and clary sage create interest in any garden.

Highlight the various foliage shades of herbs by weaving them into ribbons of color around garden structures, such as an arbor, a deck, or a tool shed. Accent an ordinary border of evergreen shrubs by sprinkling silver- and purple-leaf herbs among them.

Make an artistic statement by filling a trough, an urn, or a large container with a collection of herbs. Intersperse square patches of a creeping herb with large pavers to create a dramatic living checkerboard.

a different shade

above: **Variegated types of oregano and sage, along with green-and-white lemon thyme and society garlic, sparkle when you plant them among dark green herbs and perennials.**

classic design

right: **A wagon-wheel-shape garden makes a popular design because it's easy to plant and maintain. Fill it with varieties of one genus, such as thyme, basil, or lavender.**

brewery bound

above: Vigorous hops climbs an arbor within one season, covering it with dense foliage and pineconelike flowers by summer's end. Harvest the blooms and use them fresh to brew beer or dried to stuff dream pillows. Plant a hops variety with chartreuse foliage for even more ornamental impact.

silver spots

left: Plant a gray or silver garden for its wonderful textures and subtle yet spectacular shades. Otherwise, include silver-leaf plants throughout the garden for their ability to contrast and enthrall. Depend on artemisias alone for a stunning variety of decorative plants, from mugwort and southernwood to tarragon, 'Silver King,' and 'Powis Castle.' Combined with jagged cardoon and velvety lamb's-ears, the feathery, lacy artemisias stand out.

mighty trees

You may not think that trees qualify as herbs, but they do. The term *herb* technically includes trees, shrubs, vines, and annuals, as well as herbaceous (or fleshy) and woody perennials valued for their uses.

The utility and attractiveness of many trees merit their place in the garden. Herb trees typically yield fragrant and edible leaves, bark, or berries. They offer shade, shelter for wildlife, and year-round interest making them valuable elements in any landscape.

Trees, along with shrubs, constitute the backbone of a complete garden design. Their structure adds a vital dimension, as well as incomparable form, height, and color. Whether you choose a single, beautiful specimen or a bevy of them, include trees in your planting plans. Whether you decide to use the leaves, berries, or bark, make herb trees an integral part of your landscape.

a must-have herb

right: Call it bay, sweet bay, or bay laurel, but grow this aromatic herb for a supply of fresh leaves. Plant the tree in a pot and move it in and out of the garden where winters are cold. Keep the tree indoors or in a greenhouse or cool room during the frigid months.

remember this

left: The ginkgo tree makes a sturdy, long-lived street tree in a city or suburb setting. Its attractive fan-shape leaves rustle delightfully in a breeze. Ginkgo's furrowed bark provides winter interest after the leaves fall. Thought to be the oldest tree on the planet, ginkgo brings an Oriental feeling to a garden. It has long been used as a source of medicine, but ginkgo's effectiveness in enhancing memory and improving cerebral circulation has only recently been researched.

refreshing early bloomer

left: The yellow flowers of witch hazel appear in late winter when the landscape looks bare. These multistem shrubs or small trees win a coveted place in the landscape for their early awakening and for the stimulating, freshening astringent made from their leaves and bark. Distill the leaves and bark to use in beauty regimens or place them in a sachet to steep in your bathwater.

great herb trees

bay	linden
birch	sassafras
eucalyptus	vitex
ginkgo	willow
juniper	witch hazel

cutting gardens

gathering herbs

Include herbs in your planting scheme for a cutting garden and you will be rewarded with a variety of unusual materials for your decorative arrangements. Most people grow herbs for their leaves; their flowers are subtle and easy to overlook. However, if your focus is flowers, grow the golden buttons of tansy, the blue stars of borage, and the puffs of garlic chives. Consider growing the tall, feathery foliage and airy blossoms of dill for mixed bouquets, and other favorite bloomers, including lavender, sage, angelica, and bee balm.

If adding herbs to your cutting garden, place annuals, such as basil, dill, and parsley, where they can be pulled out at season's end without disturbing neighboring perennials.

cutting-garden design

above: A concrete urn creates a focal point for a traditional, formal design. The pathway's gray brick in a herringbone pattern contrasts with the colors of the herbs and flowers. The 6-foot-deep beds make the flowers accessible from the garden paths. Cutable blooms include germander, pineapple sage, lavender, and tansy. Sweet alyssum and pansies edge the beds.

strictly structured

left: In this four-quadrant parterre garden designed for cutting, the neat brick paths and bed edges give the garden both structure and tidiness. Myrtles, sheared into globe shapes, anchor the beds and provide year-round interest. In Zones 7 and colder, substitute a hardier evergreen shrub, such as boxwood or yew.

focus on flowers

The tried-and-true practice of harvesting culinary herbs before they flower remains a good one because it helps the plants, especially annuals, continue growing strongly rather than finishing their life cycle by producing seeds. When the flowers of annuals and perennial herbs develop, you're bound to appreciate their beauty as well as their culinary value. Gather flowers, such as chives, mint, rosemary, and sage, to use as garnishes and as striking elements in an arrangement. Other herbs with admirable blossoms include lady's mantle, feverfew, wood betony, and yarrow.

self sowing

right: **The sweet-scented white blooms of garlic chives attract butterflies and bees. Allow the seeds to develop and self sow future plants.**

edible colors

far left: The flowers of sage, basil, thyme, and feverfew create a tapestry of color in the garden and a rich harvest ready for wreath crafting.

tender beauty

left: Rosemary produces its whorls of flowers in shades of pale or dark blue, lavender, violet, pink, or white, depending on the cultivar. In warm climates, rosemary grows as a flowering shrub.

mixed company

left: Culinary herbs, such as basil, sage, and dill, team up well with colorful annuals. Dwarf French marigolds make excellent but pungent cut flowers and deter nematodes in the soil.

potted herbs

ornamental spots

Herbs need not be confined to their own garden, or any bed or border, for that matter. Give herbs a cozy home in a container and they'll reward you with their many charms. As both ornamental and practical displays, herbs in containers present options that you wouldn't have otherwise. Above all, potted herbs are portable. Place them where there is no room to garden. Use potted herbs to fill in empty spots in the garden or to decorate an outdoor living area. Keep containers of herbs on stoops and steps for convenient harvest.

practicalities

Tender perennials and tropicals that won't tolerate cold weather, such as rosemary, bay, lemongrass, and ginger, look great in pots and are easy to move indoors over winter. Containers let you

grow herbs year-round, indoors or outdoors, in combinations as changeable as the seasons or your moods. Group herbs with similar needs for soil type, sun, and water.

Contain invasive herbs, such as mint and lemon balm, to prevent them from running wild in the garden. If desired, place invasive herbs in ordinary 12-inch nursery pots and then plant them, pots and all, in the garden. Curtail the growth of other invasive herbs, such as oregano, horsetail, and comfrey, by keeping them in decorative pots and overwintering them in a protected area.

pesto in a pot
opposite: Herbs display their adaptability in containers. In this case a collection of basils represents a minigarden that thrives in a planter; the basil provides the essential ingredient for delicious pesto. The self-watering window box makes a practical way to keep plants on a patio. With the box set on pot feet, air circulates around the plants and helps keep them healthy. A water-holding reservoir built into the bottom of the planter cuts down on time spent watering.

controlling spread
left: Lemon balm, a fragrant relative of the mint family, tends to wander and take over a garden as mint does, unless you control it. Plant it in a container to keep it within bounds. Although it also tends to seed itself with abandon in surprising places, the seedlings are easy to remove.

potted herbs

outdoor oases

Whether combining multiple herbs in a large container or planting single herbs in individual pots, place them in the garden with a judicious eye toward the way they blend and contrast with each other as well as with nearby plants. Move these portable pots of color in and out of the garden, or grow an entire garden in containers, where space is limited.

For adequate room to grow, give a single plant a 6- to 12-inch pot; give a group of plants a 12- to 24-inch pot. When overcrowded, container plantings dry out quickly and require more attention to keep them going.

match mates
right: **Lemongrass, rosemary, and lavender embellish an antique birdbath in a handsome grouping of terra-cotta containers.**

tiny topiary

left: Petite standards, made with *(left to right)* English thyme, silver thyme, and scented geranium, stand in a protected spot with afternoon shade. They also grow well indoors on a sunny windowsill. Maintain the spheres by trimming new growth as it appears.

close-up scents

below left: Blue-flower heliotrope adds its cherry-pie scent to an artful planting of other fragrant herbs, including rosemary, basil, and thyme. Set the container near a door and savor the scents every time you walk by.

tiny trellis

left: A simple twig trellis adds a structural embellishment to a potted scented geranium. Without support, the plant would sprawl.

potted herbs

charming strawberry pots

Originally designed to provide a compact place for growing strawberries, these classic containers with pockets around their perimeter make ideal homes for herbs. A large strawberry pot makes an excellent focal point on a patio or a deck or in a garden. Smaller jars (6 inches in diameter) make fine tabletop planters but dry out quickly and require fastidious watering.

planting tips

Strawberry jars require a little extra attention to planting. Start by drilling ⅜-inch holes at staggered intervals in a length of PVC pipe about as tall as the pot. Stand the pipe in the center of the pot; fill it with pea gravel to keep it upright. Cover the bottom of the pot with pea gravel for drainage. Cover the gravel with soil up to the lowest pocket. Unpot an herb and slip its root ball into the pocket, spreading the roots as much as possible over the soil toward the interior of the pot. As you plant, sprinkle soil over each root ball, filling the jar to the next pocket. Place creeping and trailing plants in the side pockets; put the most upright plants in the top opening. Plant the root balls at the same level they were growing in their nursery pots. Top your planting with soil. Pour water into the pipe, letting it seep down and out into the surrounding soil. If soil leaks out while watering, poke it back into the pockets. As the plants and their roots grow, such leakage stops.

part of the picture

right: For the most satisfying results, plant the pockets of a strawberry pot with creeping, dwarf, or trailing herbs, such as the thyme and dwarf sage, *shown.* Place upright, bushy herbs, such as marjoram and common sage, in the top of the pot.

subtle presence

left: A lushly planted strawberry jar provides an outstanding focal point in a garden. Here, surrounded by herbs, nasturtiums, and foxgloves, its plump presence catches the eye without dominating the scene. Terra-cotta pots blend with a garden, while glazed ceramic containers stand out.

rich company

left: Colors, textures, and shapes combine in this strawberry pot for a rich display. Thyme and rose-scented geraniums spill out of the pockets, while purple sage and chives overflow the top. This planting looks spectacular in the center of an herb garden, on a broad-stepped walk, or next to a garden path.

potted herbs

windowsill herb gardens

Many herbs grow well indoors, whether you raise them from seeds or cuttings. They need a sunny window, such as one facing south or east. Mint, tarragon, and thyme grow well in hanging planters. Thyme makes a pretty groundcover for another potted herb, such as a bay tree. Grow a collection of your favorite culinary herbs in a narrow window box kept handy in the kitchen.

In late summer or early fall, take cuttings of herbs from the garden and overwinter them indoors. You'll have substantial-size plants ready for spring planting in the garden.

When growing herbs in pots, water them when the soil feels dry. Plastic pots hold soil moisture longer than terra-cotta pots. During winter, when the air in a heated house becomes dry, mist around the plants weekly. Symptoms of dry air include brown leaf tips and an invasion of tiny red spider mites.

Herbs produce the best flavor if you do not fertilize them, but start the plants in enriched, fertile potting soil. Give plants a quarter-turn weekly to expose all sides equally to the sun and encourage lush, even growth.

singular artistry

above right: **Plant rosemary, thyme, marjoram, and basil in separate containers to attend to the particular moisture needs of each herb. For a harmonious arrangement, use containers of the same or similar material and color, such as the terra-cotta here.**

fancy doings

right: **Make a flashy display of your herbs by potting them in colorful tomato cans from an Italian grocery. Use the cans as cachepots or drill drainage holes in their bottoms to plant directly in them.**

herbal forest

left: **A collection of small, neat herb standards makes an amazing windowsill garden. Many herbs, including scented geraniums and thyme, train easily into tiny tree forms. Rosemary and lavender make excellent standards, too. Keep an eye on the moisture level in small pots like these, especially in the dry, heated air of a room in winter. Regularly snip off leaves to keep the plants looking trim and lush. Use the leaves in cooking. Indoors, always place saucers under potted plants to protect windowsills and furniture from moisture damage.**

potting herbs

you will need

- herbs in nursery pots or seedlings in peat pots or trays
- 6-inch or larger pots: terra–cotta, fiberglass, resin, or wood
- packaged potting soil or soilless mix
- compost or composted manure
- trowel

practical points

Potting herbs takes little time and no special talent. Combining different herbs in one container, however, requires some planning. First, only plant together herbs that share cultural needs or conditions in terms of soil, light, and water. Next, consider your reason for the grouping. Show off a collection of thymes or basils, for example, or carry out a theme, such as a Mediterranean garden or plants for first aid.

Container plantings offer a convenient way to keep herbs handy, such as in or near the kitchen. Small pots nestle easily on a windowsill.

moving up

right and below: **When purchasing herbs in six-packs or other nursery pots, transplant them into roomier pots at home. These seedlings were transferred to 6-inch pots.**

plant list

1. dwarf variegated sage
2. dwarf english lavender
3. dwarf sage
4. winter savory
5. chocolate mint
6. savory
7. thyme

1 select a pot Transplant herbs into individual 6-inch pots, or opt for larger, decorative containers, which can hold several plants. Create a mini herb garden in a container that is at least 12 inches in diameter. Clay pots leach moisture from the soil, so soak them in water before potting. Soil dries faster in porous terra-cotta and clay pots than in other types of containers. However, many herbs, including those with Mediterranean origins, prefer soil that's on the dry side.

2 prepare to plant Fill the pot with potting soil or soilless mix, working in compost or composted manure; use about 1 cup of the amendment per 6-inch pot. If you mail-ordered your herb plants, carefully unwrap them. Press the potted herb into the soil to make a planting hole that's just the right size. Gently slip the young plant out of its nursery pot.

3 plant and water Gently loosen the roots at the bottom of the soil ball and set it in the planting hole. Set plants in the pot at the same level or slightly deeper than they were growing in their nursery pots. Gently press the soil around each plant. If you fill a larger pot with several plants, repeat the process for each plant. Water the soil thoroughly. If needed, top off the planting with more soil, leaving 1 inch between the top of the soil and the top of the pot (to allow for watering).

herbal window box

zones	time	skill
3–10	1–2 hours	easy

you will need

- 6 to 10 herb plants in 3-inch pots
- lightweight potting mix
- compost or composted manure
- water-retentive polymer crystals
- window box and plastic liner sized to match your windowsill
- watering can

eye-level bounty

Dress up your windows, indoors or outdoors, with a window box full of fragrant and tasty herbs. Fresh culinary herbs will be within arm's reach. Planting in a plastic liner that fits a wood, metal, or other box makes changing the plantings easy. Toward the end of the gardening season, remove annuals from the window box and compost them; transplant perennials to the garden, doing so early enough to give them time to establish themselves before winter.

handy harvests

right and below: **As soon as you finish planting, water thoroughly; allow excess water to drain before placing the liner in the window box. Water once or twice a week as needed during the growing season.**

plant list

1 rosemary
2 parsley
3 oregano
4 lavender
5 mint

1 **plan** Before planting, set the potted herbs in the window box. Arrange them as you please. Consider plant heights, as well as growth habits, such as spreading, upright, and trailing. Punch drainage holes in the bottom of the liner if there are none.

Fill the box halfway with lightweight potting mix enriched with compost or composted manure. Mix in water-retentive crystals, following directions on the package label.

2 **unpot** Unpot the plants. Gently loosen the root balls; in particular, loosen roots at the bottom of the root ball. As you set the plants in the window box, spread the roots over the soil to ensure that the roots will spread into the new soil after planting instead of continuing to encircle the root ball.

3 **plant** Set plants at the same depth they were growing in their nursery pots, spacing them about 2 inches apart. Add potting mix, filling the box and gently tamping it to settle the soil. Leave about 1 inch of space between the soil surface and the rim of the box.

Water the soil thoroughly. For best growth, set the box in an east or west window outdoors or a south window indoors.

rosemary standard

zones	time	skill
3-10	6 months	moderate

you will need

- rooted cutting of rosemary
- cell pack or peat pot
- soilless potting mix
- pruner
- 4- to 6-inch pot
- potting soil
- stake, length as desired
- plant ties or twine

standard fare

Rosemary is one of the best plants for making a standard or tree-form topiary. Its woody stem and needlelike leaves develop into a tree-like shape to grace an end table, mantel, or kitchen windowsill. To keep rosemary healthy, occasionally mist the air around plants to boost humidity. Water when soil feels dry to a depth of 2 inches.

stately fragrance

right: A rosemary standard, such as this, takes about six months to fill out and appear mature.

root Start with a rooted cutting, either one you buy or root yourself. Cut a 3- to 4-inch length of stem and strip the bottom leaves from it. Stand the cutting in a cell pack of soilless potting mix. Keep the medium moist while the stem roots. Resistance when you tug gently on the cutting, as well as new growth at the top, indicates that the plant has grown sufficient roots for transplanting.

transplant Select a container between 4 and 6 inches. (A large standard will be top heavy in a small pot.) Fill the pot with enriched potting soil. Make a depression in the soil, insert the cutting, and firm the soil around it. Set the plant in a sunny spot and let it grow until it develops side branches and triples in size (about two to three months)

stake Strip off most but not all of the lower leaves. Cut a stake to match the height desired for the finished standard and push it into the soil next to the plant. Tie the stake loosely but securely to the stem with plant ties. As the plant grows, continue to tie the stem to the stake at intervals. Let the plant continue growing for two to three months, until it reaches the desired height; then snip off the main terminal shoot.

snip and pinch Loosen the ties around the stem and stake as the trunk grows in diameter. Strip off any lower leaves that develop. Snip off stem ends to promote branching and keep errant stems from developing; use the fragrant leaves in cooking. Turn the plant clockwise weekly to give all sides of the plant equal light and to keep it growing lushly in a rounded shape.

herb garden labels

zones	time	skill
3–10	weekend	moderate

you will need

⅝-inch–diameter willow or other twigs

piece of birch bark, a cedar shake, a thin board, or metal flashing

½-inch copper nails

hammer

acrylic paint

fine artist's brush

1-inch paintbrush

polyurethane sealant

rustic settings

Natural materials belong in a garden. Whether you eventually plan to build an arbor, a fence, or a rustic table or bench from twigs and fallen trees, start with something simple, such as these garden signs. Artistic ability is not required: A few imperfections go hand in hand with the sign's rough-hewn look.

finishing touch

right: A charming plant marker is fun and easy to make.

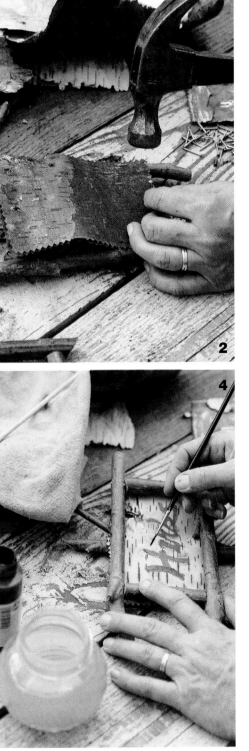

frame Gather willow or other twigs or round up prunings from your yard or a neighbor's. For best results, use straight twigs about ⅝ of an inch in diameter. Cut four pieces to make the frame: for example, two 3-inch-long pieces for the ends and two 6-inch-long pieces for the top and bottom of the frame. Cut a 12-inch-long piece for a stake. Using ½-inch copper nails, fasten the twigs together by driving each nail through a long piece and into the end of a short piece.

1

canvas Cut the piece on which you will paint from birch bark (from a fallen tree only), a cedar shake, a thin board, or metal flashing. Cut it to fit the outer dimensions of the frame. Nail the canvas to the back of the frame using copper nails.

2

stake Nail a 12-inch-long twig to the back of the frame to make a stake, allowing the top of the stake to extend an inch or two above the sign.

3

paint Using acrylic paint and a fine artist's brush, paint the name of a plant or a general term, such as "Herbs," on the sign. If you're uncomfortable painting freehand, lightly pencil in the word or words before applying the paint. Let the paint dry completely (at least 1 hour).

4

With a 1-inch paintbrush, coat the sign, including the ends of the stake, with polyurethane sealant. Let the sealant dry for at least 24 hours and then apply a second coat.

the basics

the basics

Most herbs are so easy to grow that they belong in every garden, whether in a plot of their own or mingled with perennials and shrubs. As long as you give them a well-drained site with adequate sun, herbs thrive with little attention.

start at ground level If your site doesn't drain well, raise the beds by framing them and adding soil or grow your herbs in containers. If the soil holds water, work in compost, chopped leaves, and other organic amendments each season to improve drainability.

Herbs suffer few problems with pests and diseases, thanks to the concentration of essential oils (the fragrance and flavor) in the plants.

Herbs rank among the most companionable plants because they often make an effective deterrent against insect pests when planted among other plants, especially vegetables. If pests invade, pick them off or blast them off using a strong spray from the hose. Otherwise, avoid spraying herbs with anything other than soapy water.

the easiest plants Herbs demand little but offer plenty. As with all plants, healthy herbs planted in good soil respond positively when you enrich the soil annually and support their basic needs for light and water. Herbs make easy-to-grow houseplants, too.

Established herbs tolerate dry spells; just soak the soil periodically. Transplants and immature plants need regular watering between rains to help them root and develop.

Annual herbs, which complete their life cycle within one growing season, ordinarily benefit from rich soil. Perennial herbs need winter protection in cold climates and occasional division to keep them coming back year after year. You'll minimize watering and weeding chores by mulching around your herbs.

Growing herbs is a perfect way to hone your gardening skills because they'll reward your efforts to plant seeds or cuttings by flourishing easily. Once you learn other methods of propagating plants, you'll expand your plant collection freely. Beyond that, growing herbs mainly entails harvesting their leaves and flowers and enjoying them in endless ways. Gather snips and bunches regularly before making a final harvest to last through the winter.

herb nursery

worlds of wisdom

Do you buy your herb seeds and plants, and gardening necessities and indulgences from a local nursery or a mail-order supplier? Either way, take advantage of the information and inspiration that nearby sources offer. Whether they specialize in herbs or sell a spectrum of plants, ask the staff at a garden center or nursery to help you with your garden design or to answer your herb gardening questions. Nurseries and herb farms often feature demonstration gardens, classes, and books, as well as tools and accessories. If you live near a botanical garden, take the time to meet with the knowledgeable people (perhaps members of a local herb society) who tend the herb gardens there. Most gardeners love to share their passion and practical gardening information.

real things

above: When you visit a nursery or garden center, touch and smell the plants. Buy only the plants that suit your climate and garden design. Group plants in your shopping cart or basket to get an idea of how they will look in your garden.

ideas galore

left: The demonstration gardens at many nurseries, garden centers, and herb farms display planting ideas, as well as ways to use edging, mulch, statuary, and other ornamentation. This herb bed expresses the design concept with an iron frame. Take the idea further by planting an old bed frame with herbs that are said to bolster sleep, such as chamomile, hops, valerian, and lavender.

starting seeds

1 sprinkle Fill individual pots or a flat of six-packs or cells with moistened commercial seed-starting mix. Sprinkle seeds lightly on soil, following directions on the seed packet; sow one seed or two in each cell or pocket of a six-pack. Cover the seeds with about ⅛ inch of the mix. Press the mix down lightly and spritz the surface with water to moisten it and settle the seeds.

Sow borage, chervil, coriander, dill, and fennel in warm garden soil because they don't transplant well.

2 cover up Keep the mix moist by covering the container with plastic wrap or a plastic bag; cover a six-pack or flat with a plastic dome. Remove the covering when seedlings emerge. Place the container in a sunny (south-facing) window. Keep the mix evenly moist by watering it from the bottom: Set the containers in a sink filled with 2 inches of water until beads of moisture appear on the soil surface. When the seedlings reach 2 inches tall, transplant them into individual pots or thin those started in small pots to one per pot by snipping off all but the strongest-looking one.

great herbs to start from seed

angelica	fennel
basil	lemon balm
borage	marjoram
chamomile	parsley
chives	sage
chervil	stevia
cilantro/coriander	thyme
dill	winter savory

plants from cuttings

snip cutting Propagate cuttings from new growth in spring or early fall. Cut 3- to 4-inch stems using a sharp pruner, a knife, or shears. Make the cut at an angle just below a node (where a leaf emerges from the stem). Pinch off the bottom leaves and any flowers or buds.

1

plant in pot Dip cut ends in a rooting hormone powder to help them grow. Stand cuttings 1 inch deep in a loose, sterile soil or soilless mix in the cells of seedling flats or in individual pots.

2

keep moist Cover the plantings with a sheet of plastic or a dome to help keep the soil moist; prop open the cover to let air circulate among the cuttings. Place the cuttings in bright light but out of direct sunlight.

3

In four to six weeks, transfer them to 6-inch pots or transplant them in the garden.

Alternatively: Root cuttings in a glass of water set on a sunny windowsill. Periodically add fresh water and replace it if it looks cloudy. Plant well-rooted cuttings in soil.

great herbs for cuttings

bay	lemon verbena
borage	mint
catnip	rosemary
feverfew	sage
germander	scented geranium
hyssop	tarragon
lavender	thyme
lemon balm	winter savory

dividing herbs

1 **dig up** Divide plants in early spring or late fall when they are dormant (resting, not growing). Plants that grow in clumps, such as chives (*shown*), and those that increase via underground runners, such as mint, make good candidates for division.

Dig up an entire plant or slice through the parent plant and take one section.

2 **cut** Divide the plant using a sharp knife or spade. Insert the tool into the middle of the plant and cut it in half. Repeat the process to divide a plant into quarters, eighths, or smaller sections. Each division must have roots and shoots. Some herbs, such as chives and lemongrass, divide easily by gently pulling them apart.

For herbs that produce shoots from underground runners, such as mint and catnip, dig up the new plants and treat them as young transplants.

3 **replant** Immediately plant new divisions to prevent their roots from drying out. If you cannot replant right away, keep the roots moist. Set the plants out of direct sun until you transplant them.

great herbs for dividing

artemisia	lemon balm	sorrel
bee balm	lemongrass	sweet woodruff
catnip	marjoram	tansy
chives	mint	tarragon
hyssop	oregano	thyme
lady's mantle	rosemary	valerian
lavender	rue	winter savory

layering herbs

nick stem Layering represents the easiest method of propagation. Woody perennials, such as sage (*shown*) and lavender, make excellent candidates for layering.

   In late spring or early summer, select a healthy, flexible stem and gently pull it to the ground or a pot of soil set near the parent plant. Remove the foliage from the section you want to root; then use a small, sharp knife to nick the underside of the stem in several places where it will touch the soil.

use rooting hormone To bolster root formation, dust the nicks with a rooting hormone powder.

press in soil Carefully lay the stem on the soil. Lightly cover the treated section of the stem with soil, leaving about 6 inches of the tip end unburied. Anchor the stem to the soil using a brick that will help preserve the soil moisture; or use 4-inch lengths of wire bent into U-shape pins.

   Water the soil and keep it moist until roots develop (in about six weeks).

   When a sufficient root system develops, cut the stem to detach it from the parent plant and transplant the new plant where you wish it to grow.

great herbs for layering

catnip	sage
lavender	santolina
lemon verbena	tarragon
marjoram	thyme
rosemary	winter savory

planting tips

1 **crowd control** Some herbs become invasive, crowd other plants, and even take over a garden. Tansy (*shown*), catnip, comfrey, horseradish, lemon balm, hops, artemisia, all kinds of mint, and other herbs spread aggressively via underground runners unless you control them. Curtail invasive herbs by planting each one in a 12-inch nursery pot and then submerging the pot in the ground. The pot won't be visible but it will help keep the plant in bounds.

2 **mint in barrels** No collection of herbs would be complete without mint, a fragrant yet invasive herb. Prevent them from completely taking over the garden by planting them in half-barrels or containers. Create an attractive design by planting a different mint variety in each container, such as orange, ginger, peppermint, spearmint, and chocolate mint.

3 **a tisket, a tasket** Recycle an old or damaged basket into a pretty planter at the edge of the garden. Fill the basket with soil and then use it to nursery tender herb seedlings until they are large enough (at least 6 inches tall) to transplant into the garden or a larger container. Or sprinkle a variety of herb seeds over the soil and transplant the seedlings when they reach at least 6 inches tall.

here and there Whether you're designing a new garden or filling holes in an established one, herbs offer endless planting potential. The best times to plant are in spring, after the soil has warmed, or in early fall.

Make herbs an integral part of your plans for nonstop blooms. Planted next to spring-blooming bulbs, for example, chives and sage reach their peak and bloom just in time to cover up the dying foliage of hyacinths and daffodils. Stagger plantings of basil and dill from early to midsummer and enjoy fresh herbs into fall.

Use graceful, mounding plants, such as chives, lady's mantle, or parsley, along edges of beds and garden paths. Tuck creeping thyme between stepping-stones or upright thyme into pockets of a rock garden.

great herbs for planting in full sun

basil	lavender
chives	oregano
cilantro/coriander	parsley
comfrey	rosemary
dill	sage
fennel	salad burnet

great herbs for planting in partial shade

angelica	lemon balm
bee balm	lovage
catnip	mint
chervil	sweet cicely
feverfew	sweet violet
hyssop	sweet woodruff
lady's mantle	wintergreen

maintenance

1   **pinching** Whether you grow herbs outdoors or indoors, keep the plants lush and bushy by regularly pinching 2 to 3 inches off the tips. If you desire more leaves, pinch off any flowers that form. When transplanting, remove the top two leaves from each plant to encourage root growth.

2   **fertilizing and mulching** Herbs grow best in well-drained soil. Unless you already have the alkaline or sandy soil that herbs tolerate, throw a handful each of sand, powdered lime, and powdered gypsum into every planting hole. If you have clay soil or extremely sandy ground, add compost and chopped leaves each season.

At planting time and each spring, build the soil by scratching in 3 inches of compost and rotted manure. If plants appear weak, pale, or otherwise unhealthy, give them a drink of diluted fish fertilizer. Feed potted herbs every two to three weeks.

Too much fertilizer (particularly nitrogen) results in lots of green leaves without much fragrance or flavor.

Lay a 2-inch layer of mulch, such as cocoa bean hulls or wood chips, on bare ground between plants to suppress weeds and help preserve soil moisture. Replace mulch as it decomposes.

If you live in a cold climate, use chopped leaf mulch to help protect plants over winter. After the ground freezes, lay a 4-inch layer of leaves around plants. Lay evergreen boughs over gray-leaf herbs, which need extra protection from the cold.

spring pruning Prune and clean up dead stems of last year's growth on plants, such as lemon balm, mint, artemisia, and tansy that weren't cut back in autumn. Some perennial herbs become woody or lanky after several years in the garden. In spring, prune them back by one-third before new growth begins in order to encourage bushy, more compact overall forms, as well as more foliage and flowers.

3

Do not prune woody perennials, such as lavender, santolina, and germander: They develop new growth on the woody stems that grew the previous year. Lavender plants mature over their first three years. Avoid cutting the plants; cut only the flowers. After plants turn green in spring, trim off only dead (gray) plant parts.

fall cleanup After the first frost in fall, pull up spent annual plants, such as calendula, dill, cilantro, and chervil. Shake the soil off their roots, leaving it in the garden, and toss the plant remains on the compost pile.

4

Many gardeners prefer to leave the remains of perennial plants in the garden over winter. The stems catch leaves and snow that provide a natural blanket for the plant during the cold months. After the weather warms in spring and perennial herbs start to show new growth, trim off any dead parts and compost them.

harvesting

1   **summer cuts** Throughout summer, snip plants regularly to encourage branching and new growth. Harvest successive cuttings whenever you need fresh herbs. Generally, cut no more than one-third of the stem's length. Exceptions include chives and lavender: When they bloom, harvest the flowering stems at ground level.

Use the snippets of culinary herbs in cooking. Use other fresh herbs to make bouquets and teas or for a delightful herbal bath.

2   **harvest handfuls** Gather herbs early in the day, after the dew has dried but before the sun bakes the plants' essential oils. If you're harvesting an herb's leaves, cut the stems at their peak, when the flowers start to form. If you like, gather the blooms of herbs when they develop fully. If you're after an herb's seeds, wait until they mature and begin to turn brown before harvesting the seed heads.

3

4

5

strip leaves To prepare leafy stems for use in cooking, strip the leaves off the stems by sliding your thumb and forefinger from top to bottom. Snip off thicker leaves, such as those of parsley, bay, or tansy, which don't strip off readily. If you plan to remove the herbs before serving the food, skip stripping and use whole stems. Tie them together for easier removal from whatever you are cooking.

3

herb bunches The traditional way to preserve herbs entails gathering small bunches of 10 to 15 stems and hanging them in a warm, airy place to dry. Wrap stems tightly with a rubber band or tie them with twine. Hang the bunches on a drying rack, on the rung of a hanger, or from a nail. Drying can take up to three weeks, depending on the plant and its moisture content. Strip crisp-dry leaves off stems before storing them.

4

Dry seed heads by placing a paper bag over them and tying it shut around the stems. Place only one type of herb in each bag and label it. The seeds will drop into the bag as they dry. Let seeds dry for several weeks before storing them properly.

proper storage Store dried herbs in airtight glass or ceramic containers away from light and heat (never on or near the stove) to protect their flavor and fragrance. Keep the leaves whole until used (crushing leaves releases their flavor). Use dried herbs within a year of harvesting.

5

bringing plants indoors

1 **extend the season** Growing herbs indoors lets you enjoy the delights of fresh-picked herbs year-round. As summer ends, transplant herbs from the garden to pots and move them indoors. Select plants, including immature annuals or tender perennials, and dig carefully around their roots to avoid damaging them. Annuals, such as this basil, will continue growing into winter. Return perennials to the garden in spring.

2 **pot 'em up** Select a container large enough to accommodate a plant's root ball, allowing room for growth. Leave some garden soil on the plant's root ball. Partially fill the pot with potting soil. Set the root ball on top of the soil; fill in around it with more soil. Water thoroughly. Leave your newly potted plants outdoors in a lightly shaded location for about a week to help them begin acclimating to their new home.

Before you bring plants indoors, inspect them thoroughly for hitchhiking insects. Flush the soil with water and rinse off the foliage, using a blast of water from the garden hose to chase away any pests and avoid later problems.

3 **perennial goodness** If you live in a frost zone, keep tender perennial herbs going from year to year by bringing them indoors over winter. Lemongrass (*shown*), ginger, bay, rosemary, scented geranium, and lemon verbena, for example, require protection from cold weather to survive. Also bring in lavender, tricolor sage, pineapple sage, and heliotrope.

4

extra-special care Rosemary, a tender perennial, can grow year-round in a container. To raise it successfully indoors, be sure to circumvent the dry air that develops in heated homes during winter. Watering often is not the answer: Constantly wet soil damages rosemary's roots. Instead, mist frequently around the plant to help raise the humidity level and also help deter red spider mites, which are the bane of rosemary grown indoors.

5

windowsill wonders When bringing your herb plants indoors, expect them to adjust during the first few weeks. Plants typically drop a few leaves and grow more slowly. Help plants acclimate to life indoors and thrive during winter by placing them in a window that receives at least six hours of sun daily. Pinch off the tips of stems periodically to stimulate lush growth. Water when the soil feels dry to a depth of 1 inch. Mist the air around plants once a week to boost the humidity level.

great herbs for growing indoors

aloe	hyssop	parsley
basil	lemon balm	rosemary
borage	lemon verbena	sage
calendula	lemongrass	scented geranium
chervil	marjoram	
chives	mint	sweet bay
ginger	oregano	thyme

from the
garden

from the
garden

Growing in the garden, herbs have only begun to fulfill their purpose. Once you gather them in snippets and bundles, you'll be on the time-worn path to discovering their amazingly diverse uses beyond the garden.

herbs for all uses Whether your forte is decorating, cooking, or crafting, explore the myriad possibilities that herbs inspire in all these areas, in addition to their prospects for bolstering your well-being. You plant lavender in your garden for its graceful beauty, for instance, but when you gather the flowers and leaves and inhale their perfume, you relax. Lavender's soothing yet refreshing fragrance

surrounds you as you transform the plant materials into lavender water, bath herbs, potpourri, and even delectable cookies. The intriguing flavors of herbs offer a complex realm of familiar and new, mouth-watering and healthful. Next thing you know, you'll be gathering a variety of herbs and making sweet-scented sachets to tuck into closets and dresser drawers. Their scent will take you back to the garden for months to come. Your friends and family will also enjoy your handcrafted herbal gifts of wreaths, vinegar, pesto, and mustard—all fresh from the garden. You'll find great pleasure and pride in getting to know herbs and putting them to use, fresh or dried, as people have for centuries in endless ways.

unlimited possibilities A simple bouquet of herbs perfumes the air. While the herbs' foliage presents a tapestry of textures and subtle colors, the blooms offer a beautiful bonus. Let bouquets do double-duty, first as pretty decoration, and then as part of culinary delicacies. Gather armloads of herbs to fashion into gorgeous wreaths, swags, or old-fashioned tussie-mussies, which speak volumes in the traditional language of herbs. Before long, you'll be blending other pretty and fragrant concoctions for your home. You'll take special delight in making your own herbal cosmetics, harvesting bundles of your favorite culinary herbs for kitchen wreaths, and snipping their delicate blooms for superb, colorful garnishes. The world of cooking with herbs awaits you with aromatic baked goods, piquant condiments, a perfect cup of tea, and more.

HERBS OF PROVENCE
makes ½ c.

3 TBS dried marjoram
3 TBS. dried thyme
3 TBS. dried summer savory
1 TBS. dried sweet basil
1½ teas. dried rosemary, crumb
1½ teas. dried sage, crushed
½ teas. fennel seeds

Combine herbs, mix well, & pack
into airtight container. Store
in a cool dark place up to 6 mo.

fresh-herb wreath

zones	time	skill
4–10	2 hours	moderate

you will need

- sphagnum sheet moss
- 18-inch concave wire wreath form
- floral U-shape pins
- potting soil
- water-retentive polymer crystals
- herbs in six-packs or 3-inch pots
- annual flowers in six-packs (optional)
- green spool wire
- sturdy hook or nail

decorative herbs

Wreaths festooned with living herbs make wonderful decorations indoors and out. Better yet, a culinary herb wreath provides a continual source of fresh herbs for cooking. Hang the herbal wreath on a wall near the kitchen or grill, where it looks great and is convenient for frequent pinching and use.

Combine plantings of herbs with colorful flowers, such as alyssum and lobelia. To keep your living wreath in good shape, pinch the tips of the herbs when you plant them and regularly after that. Occasionally clip errant stems and trim the wreath overall to keep it growing lush and looking good. Use the herb clippings in cooking.

Whether you use annual or perennial herbs, enjoy the wreath for the duration of the growing season and compost the plants in autumn. Alternatively, bring the wreath indoors, set it on a tray in a sunny place, and enjoy it as long as it continues to grow well.

Water the wreath every 10 days or so by taking it down and soaking it in a tub of water.

living wreath

right: Small transplants of sage, parsley, and marjoram, for example, add color and texture to a wreath. Thyme and prostrate rosemary grow well in a wreath if the stems are pinned to the moss as they spread.

1 **fill** Soak fresh or dried sphagnum sheet moss in a bucket of water for a few minutes. Work on a flat surface, such as an outdoor table, that won't be damaged by water and dirt. Squeeze excess water from a piece of sheet moss. Line an 18-inch wire wreath form with generous pieces of moss, overlapping the pieces slightly, and letting them drape over the sides of the frame. Press the moss into the frame, making room to add potting soil.

Moisten potting soil and combine it with water-retentive polymer crystals, following package directions.

2 **plant** Mound the damp soil in the center of the moss as high as possible. Unpot plants and spread their roots on the soil. Space the plants 3 inches or so apart, working around the ring and alternating plants for variety. Pull moss up around the soil balls of the plants and pin the moss in place using U-shape pins (available from florist or crafts suppliers). Tuck in additional moss to cover any bare spots, securing with U-shape pins.

Wrap green spool wire around the wreath, working from the outside to the inside of the ring and winding around from front to back. Lift only the part of the wreath that you are wrapping. Wrap the entire wreath. Twist the wire ends together. Water thoroughly. Use a strong hook or nail to hang the wreath.

dried herb wreath

zones	time	skill
3–10	2 hours	easy

you will need

- straw wreath base
- dried herbs
- dried fruits, whole spices (optional)
- U-shape floral pins, green floral wire
- glue gun, glue sticks

hang around

Add a personal touch to any wall with a handmade wreath. Delicately fragrant wreaths also make lovely, unusual centerpieces. Create this one using U-shape floral pins or hot glue to secure dried fruit, whole spices, and bay leaves to a straw wreath base. Add small bundles of herbs by wrapping them with wire, leaving a 2-inch tail of wire to slip into the wreath.

incredibly edible

right: Make a pretty culinary wreath using bay leaves, cinnamon sticks, dried fruits, dried hot peppers, and garlic bulbs. Use the herbs and spices in cooking, if desired.

hang 'em high

left: Hang bunches of herbs to dry for use later in a variety of projects, such as composing wreaths or culinary blends. To preserve their fragrance and color, hang bunches upside down in a warm, dry, and airy place away from light and heat. Use bunches of marjoram, tansy, artemisia, sage, and lavender, along with roses and statice, as rustic decor.

herbal greeting

left: Use a variety of colorful, dried herbs and flowers to create a welcoming wreath. Here, chive blossoms, sage, artemisia, yarrow, and spikes of lavender encircle a wreath. Indoors, hang wreaths away from light and heat to preserve their colors. Avoid hanging a delicate wreath on a door where it might be bumped, banged, and damaged.

herb swag

zones	time	skill
3–10	weekend	moderate

you will need

20–gauge wire

wire cutter

spanish moss

glue gun, glue sticks

small bunches and stems of fragrant herbs and flowers

pruner

2 yards of translucent ribbon

floral sealer (optional)

make a swag

First, gather herbs and flowers in a broad mix of colors, textures, and fragrances. Adjust the size of the swag to fit the back of the chair you choose. Make a set of swags to hang on all your dining chairs.

bloomin' simple

right and opposite: **Decorate a fragrant swag with colorful blooms of herbs, such as artemisia, tansy, sage, and lavender. Flowers might include roses, larkspur, and statice. Hang the swag on a chair back or wall.**

1 **make frame** Cut a 7-foot length of wire. Make a loop the size of a teaspoon at one end of the wire. Bend the rest of the wire into a wide U-shape large enough to cover the back of the chair. Make another teaspoon-size loop at the other end of the swag, and then double the wire back over the U to give the frame extra support. Twist the wire ends to secure them.

2 **add herbs** Starting in the middle of the U, attach Spanish moss to the frame using a glue gun. Work out toward the ends, covering both front and back but not the loops. Cut herbs into 2- to 3-inch-long pieces. Dab hot glue on the stem ends of the foliage first and then the flowers; insert them into the moss. Secure them to the moss with the glue gun.

3 **finish** As you add the herbs, alternate them to get a mixed look with varied colors and textures from both foliage and flowers.

Cut ribbon in half; thread each half through the wire loop on each end of the swag. Tie the swag to the chair back with the ribbon. To protect the swag, spray it with a floral sealer (available in crafts supply stores) if desired.

herb bouquets

double duty

Herbs go from the garden to the table, where they do double duty as bouquets or gifts, and then as ingredients in cooking. Take advantage of the colors, textures, and forms of both herb foliage and flowers by adding them as accents to your flower arrangements or gathering them into their own beautiful and aromatic bunches. Most herbs air-dry well after they've served as a bouquet; let them stand in the vase without water. They'll still be useful in cooking as dried material.

tussie-mussies

Embellish a gift package or place setting with a special nosegay of herbs and flowers and use their traditional meanings to send a message at the same time. For example, lemon balm stands for sympathy; mint = wisdom; parsley = festivity; rosemary = remembrance; and sage = esteem and long life. Use the herbs and flowers from your garden to make a pretty, conversational keepsake. Gather a small bunch of fresh or dried herbs and tie the stems with ribbon or raffia, or arrange them in a chunk of floral foam that holds water. Make a package decoration using a half-sphere floral foam holder with an adhesive bottom (available at crafts and florist's suppliers).

traditional posy

above right: **This heartwarming gift topper combines lamb's-ears, tansy, rosemary, lavender, globe amaranth, and statice, all secured to a core of floral foam.**

holiday bouquet

right: **To flavor a Thanksgiving feast, arrange cut herbs, such as sage, chives, garlic chive blossoms, purple basil, and dill, in low jars filled with water to keep them fresh. Or, combine cut and potted herbs. Set the herbs in a basket.**

graceful design

left: The lacy foliage and airy yellow flowers of dill make charming, informal arrangements. Use dill alone or combine the leaves and flowers with basil and garlic chives. Add stems of curly-leaf parsley to create a pretty salad bouquet. Sow dill more than once in a season; using some of the harvest for table decorations won't deplete your supply.

kitchen bouquet

below: Although you usually want to harvest basil leaves before the plants flower, the spiky blossoms make aromatic and delightful additions to arrangements. If you cut the flowers just as they begin to open, the plants will continue to produce leaves. Mix purple and common green basils together. Use the leaves in Italian cuisine, on sandwiches, and in salads. Sprinkle the blossoms on soups, salads, or pasta.

culinary herbs

herbs in the kitchen

When you begin cooking with herbs, select a single herb and explore its flavors by using it alone in various dishes. When you reach familiarity and discover your preferences, experiment with different combinations. Depending on the herb and the dish, use whole sprigs of fresh herbs, torn or minced leaves, or a paste (ground in a mortar and pestle). Crush dried herbs between your palms or fingers. Add them to a dish one pinch at a time, to avoid overseasoning.

Add mild-flavor herbs, such as parsley and basil, near the end of the cooking process to preserve their flavors. Add strong-flavor ones, such as rosemary and sage, at the beginning of the cooking process.

Blend classic combinations of herbs, such as herbs of Provençe (see *page 89*) and bouquet garni, which add complex flavors to stocks, stews, vegetables, and roasts. Make bouquet garni with fresh or dried chervil or parsley, bay leaf, thyme, and marjoram. Tie the blend into a cheesecloth bundle and place it in the dish; remove the bundle before serving. Make fines herbes for delicate cheese-and-egg dishes, as well as savory sauces by blending equal parts of minced fresh parsley, tarragon, chives, and chervil.

Pesto highlights the intense flavors of herbs in a fine paste that can be served many ways. Classic pesto features fresh basil with Parmesan cheese, pine nuts, and olive oil. Vary your pesto, using another herb, cheese, nut, and oil.

a classic use

right: **If you love basil, you'll adore classic pesto, which marries biting garlic to aromatic basil. Store pesto in the freezer in individual portions to toss into soup or stew near the end of the cooking process.**

perfect pesto

Toss pesto with just-cooked, drained pasta; or spread it on bread.

1 cup firmly packed fresh basil (leaves only)
½ cup firmly packed parsley sprigs (stems removed)
½ cup grated Parmesan or Romano cheese
½ cup pine nuts, walnuts, or almonds
1 large clove garlic (or to taste), quartered
¼ teaspoon salt (optional)
¼ cup olive oil or cooking oil

In a blender container or food-processor bowl, combine all ingredients except olive oil. Cover and blend until a paste forms, using an on-off pulse and stopping several times to scrape the sides of the bowl. With the machine on slow, add olive oil and blend until the pesto reaches the consistency of soft butter. Use pesto immediately; refrigerate for up to 2 days or freeze for up to 6 months.

spicy basil

above: **Both common green- and purple-leaf basils make tasty additions to various foods, and pesto concentrates their flavors.**

terrific teas

Tea refreshes, whether served steaming hot on a cold winter night or served frosty cold on a sweltering summer day. Whether you grow and harvest a few herbs that happen to make tasty tea or plant an entire garden intended for the teapot, you'll find pleasure in exploring the subtle flavors of herbs as well as ways to serve them. Garnishing hot and cold drinks with sprigs of fresh herbs offers another way to enjoy their delicate scents and flavors.

how to make a perfect cup of tea

A proper cup of hot tea refreshes and perks your senses with its delicious warmth and aroma. Make hot tea in a glass, ceramic, or porcelain (not metal) pot. Most herbal teas are made from leaves and flowers in an infusion: Pour 1 cup of boiling water over 3 teaspoons of fresh herbs or 1 teaspoon of dried herbs for each cup of tea. When making a pot of tea, add an extra teaspoon of herbs for the pot (an old tradition that improves the flavor of the tea). Cover and let steep for 5 to 10 minutes. Strain out the herbs using a bamboo tea strainer. Serve plain or with a bit of honey and a slice of lemon.

Use herbs singly or in combination, depending on your preference. Experiment!

great herbs for tea

anise hyssop	lemon balm
bee balm	lemon verbena
chamomile	lemongrass
cinnamon basil	mint
fennel	sage

tea time
opposite: Served hot, lemon verbena tea is perfect for a tea party or dessert. Use fresh sprigs of the herb as an aromatic garnish.

refreshing thirst quencher
left: Serve icy lemonade or tea with a sprig of peppermint or spearmint. Both herbs tickle your nose and wake up your taste buds.

delicious duos
below left: Combine single-herb teas with fruit juices to make delightful beverages. Blend pineapple sage, mint, or ginger with pineapple juice; rosemary with cranberry juice; and chamomile with apple juice.

refreshing sun tea

    1- to 2-quart jar
   1 cup crushed mint leaves, loosely packed
  ¹⁄₂ cup crushed lemon balm leaves, loosely packed
   6 tea bags (regular or decaffeinated)
    cold water
  ¹⁄₂ lemon, thinly sliced
  ¹⁄₂ lime, thinly sliced
  ¹⁄₂ orange, thinly sliced
    sugar (optional)

Rinse herbs. Place the herbs and tea bags in the jar. Fill with water to within 4 inches of the jar's top. Set it in the sun for 2 to 3 hours. Stir and strain.

Add citrus slices. Place the jar in the refrigerator for several hours until chilled. Stir before serving over ice in tall glasses with a few fruit slices in each glass. Sweeten with sugar, if desired.

This recipe works equally well for iced tea you make indoors. The only difference is that you pour boiling water over the herb leaves and tea bags instead of letting the heat of the sun do the work. Steep for 20 minutes; then strain and refrigerate.

grilled perfection

Grilling with herbs is as simple as tossing several fresh sprigs (or pinches, if dried) of rosemary, thyme, or a favorite herb onto hot coals. The herb exudes its aroma as the fish, meat, or other food cooks. Tie together sprigs of fresh herbs and use them as a basting brush, dipping the leaves in oil or a marinade and then brushing the food while grilling. For year-round use, blend dried herbs into mixes, such as this one for seafood, *right*, which contains lavender, thyme, bay, rosemary, lemon verbena, dill, and fennel.

herb vinegars

Fresh herbs flavor salad dressings and marinades when steeped in vinegar.

Loosely fill 1-quart glass jars with about 3 tablespoons of fresh herbs–individually or in combination. Add vinegar (white wine, apple cider, or your choice) to cover. Secure lid and steep for 1 to 2 months in a cool, dark place. Strain vinegar through cone-shape paper coffee filters. Pour into clean, sterilized bottles. Cork tightly and label.

flavorful blends

above right: **Blend enough savory grilling herbs to keep on hand and give to friends.**

zesty marinades

right: **Herb vinegars make delectable marinades and salad dressings. They also make great gifts.**

luscious refreshment

opposite: **Lemon herb and fruit flavors combine for a cooling dessert.**

great herbs for herb vinegars

basil	marjoram	salad burnet
bay	mint	savory
cayenne	oregano	tarragon
chives	rosemary	thyme
lemon thyme		

lemon thyme ice

This icy treat, a welcome sight on hot summer days, can be made up to a week in advance. Prep: 30 minutes. Cook: 5 minutes. Freeze: up to 1 week.

  3 cups water
  1 cup sugar
  1 teaspoon finely shredded lemon peel
  ½ cup fresh lemon juice
  1 tablespoon snipped fresh lemon thyme or dried lemon, finely crushed
  4 drops yellow food coloring (optional)
    sliced or cooked fruit
    lemon thyme sprigs (optional)

In a medium saucepan combine the water, sugar, and, if using, dried thyme. Bring just to boiling to dissolve sugar; remove from heat. Stir in lemon peel. Cool thoroughly. Cover and chill.

In a 2-quart square baking dish, combine the chilled syrup mixture, lemon juice, and, if using, fresh lemon thyme. Add yellow food coloring, if desired. Cover and freeze about 3 to 4 hours or until almost firm.

Break the frozen mixture into small chunks. Transfer chunks to a chilled mixing bowl. Beat with an electric mixer on medium speed until mixture is fluffy but not melted. Return quickly to the chilled dish. Cover and freeze until firm. Store covered in the refrigerator for up to 1 week.

To serve, if the mixture is very firm, let it stand at room temperature for 5 minutes. Scrape across the top of the ice to form 2-inch balls. Place a ball of the ice on top of sliced fresh fruit. Garnish with lemon thyme sprigs, if desired. Makes about 4½ cups or 9 servings.

taste sensations

Preserve the peak flavors of herbs in enticing jellies.
Vary the ingredients (but not the quantities) to
produce a myriad of tasty combinations. Blend apple
juice with mint, cherry juice with lavender, or apricot
nectar with cinnamon basil, for example. For headier
flavors, substitute wine for juice, blending white wine
with cilantro or red wine with rosemary. Use the
jellies as spreads on bread or crackers; or glaze
chicken and vegetables with them.

For a different taste sensation, make your own
mustard with dried spices and mustard seeds collected
from the cheerful but aggressive mustard plant.

mint jelly with orange

   2 cups freshly squeezed orange juice
   1 cup fresh spearmint leaves, loosely packed
   4 cups sugar
   ¼ cup apple cider vinegar or lemon juice
   3 tablespoons liquid pectin
   4 pint jars or 8 half-pint jars

In a nonaluminum saucepan, bring the juice to a
boil; pour over mint. Steep for 20 to 30 minutes.
Use a strainer or paper coffee filter to strain juice,
pressing mint to strain thoroughly. Return liquid
to saucepan. Add sugar and vinegar or lemon
juice. Bring to a boil; boil until sugar dissolves.
Stir in pectin and return to a rolling boil. Stir for
1 minute. Remove from heat; skim off any foam.
Pour into sterile jelly jars. Place jars in a kettle
covered with 1 inch of hot water; bring to a boil
and boil for 5 minutes. Use canning tongs to
remove jars from the water bath; place jars on a
rack. Cool completely without disturbing jars.
Makes about four 8-ounce jars.

enticing treats
right: **Herbal jellies and jams capture the
aromatic qualities of herbs in their delicate,
sweet flavors.**

classic dijon mustard

Make your own spicy French mustard with this surprisingly easy recipe.

1¼ cups brown mustard seeds
  1 cup dry mustard
  1 cup water
  1 cup distilled vinegar
  ¼ cup dry white wine
  7 cloves garlic, minced
  3 tablespoons white wine Worcestershire sauce
  1 teaspoon ground allspice
  1 teaspoon sugar
2¼ teaspoons salt
  ¼ teaspoon turmeric
  ¼ teaspoon ground white pepper
  ¼ teaspoon ground mace
  ⅛ teaspoon ground cinnamon

In a nonaluminum container, combine seeds, dry mustard, water, vinegar, and wine. Cover. Soak for 48 hours; add water, vinegar, and wine (if necessary, in correct proportions) to keep seeds covered. Stir at least once a day.

Transfer to a food-processor. Add garlic; process until creamy and seed-flecked (about 6 minutes). Add enough water, vinegar, and wine (in correct proportions) to make creamy; it will thicken slightly upon standing.

Transfer to a 2-quart crockery cooker. Cover. Cook on low heat for 4 hours, maintaining temperature of 130° to 140°. Do not simmer. Stir five times during first hour; stir occasionally during remaining time. Press through a fine-mesh metal strainer. Transfer to a nonaluminum container. Stir in remaining ingredients. Cover and store in refrigerator for up to 6 months. After 3 to 4 weeks, the flavor mellows and improves. Makes about 1¾ cups.

mustard mélange

above: **Herbs as varied as basil and dill add flavor to tasty homemade mustards.**

grow your own

left: **The mustard plant grows wild in North America. Small clusters of yellow flowers mature into narrow, seed-filled pods.**

culinary herbs

herb butters and cheeses

A great way to become familiar with the flavor of an herb entails making an herb butter or herb cheese and using it as a spread. Blend 2 teaspoons of chopped fresh herb with ¼ cup of butter or cream cheese. Let stand at room temperature for 30 minutes. Spread it on crackers or bread, corn on the cob, grilled or cooked vegetables, or pasta.

    Almost any herb makes a delicious herb butter. Some of the best are parsley, chives, savory, marjoram, garlic chives, lemon balm, tarragon, and chervil. These herbs also lend special aromas and seasonings to cheeses. Blend the herbs with semisoft or soft cheese brought to room temperature. Add shredded hard cheese and shape the cheese blend into balls, tubes, or rectangles. Chill before serving. Topping a cheese slice with an herb sprig or leaf makes for a special hors d'oeuvre.

herbal canapés

right: Spread crackers with a soft cheese, such as Brie or Camembert, and top with sprigs of parsley, rosemary, or dill and an edible flower.

buttery goodness

below: Herb butters transform snacks into hors d'oeuvres. Serve chilled butter in a stoneware bowl embellished with edible flowers and chopped fresh herbs (the same herbs that are blended in the butter).

herb butter

  1 cup butter (preferably sweet, unsalted), softened
  1 tablespoon snipped fresh herb, such as thyme,
    savory, parsley, basil, or chives

In a small bowl, thoroughly combine butter and herb (choose one or more herbs). Spoon butter into a small decorative bowl or shape it into a 1-inch-diameter log and wrap it in plastic wrap. Chill it about 3 hours. Store unused butter in the refrigerator or the freezer.

great edible herb blossoms

basil	nasturtium	spearmint
chives	oregano	thyme
lavender	pineapple sage	
lemon thyme	rosemary	
marjoram	sage	

peppered herb cheese ball

8-ounce package cream cheese

4-ounce package goat cheese

2 tablespoons chives, snipped fresh

2 tablespoons basil, snipped fresh

1 teaspoon caraway seed, crushed

1 clove garlic, minced

1 tablespoon peppercorns, pink or green, crushed

1 tablespoon parsley, snipped fresh

Assorted crackers

In a medium bowl, combine cream cheese and goat cheese until smooth. Stir in remaining ingredients, except peppercorns and parsley. Form into a ball. Chill for 30 minutes. Roll ball in crushed peppercorns and parsley. Serve with crackers. Chill for up to 24 hours or serve immediately. Makes 1½ cups.

cheesy choice

left: Herb cheese balls make great gifts. Freeze them to have on hand for company.

added attractions

Bakers have long infused their breads, muffins, tarts, and other goodies with the savory flavors of herbs. The tradition of baking with herbs continues today, with favored aromatic ingredients ranging from scented geranium, thyme, and rosemary to oregano, chives, and basil. Add individual herbs or judicious combinations to your favorite bread recipes or to packaged bread mixes. Delicious blends of herbs include dill and savory; chives, marjoram, and thyme; basil, parsley, and oregano; and lemon thyme and lemon balm.

tiny tea cookies

2 eggs
1 stick (½ cup) butter
1 cup sugar
1½ cups flour
2 teaspoons baking powder
½ teaspoon salt
1 teaspoon minced lavender, tarragon, or lemon verbena leaves; or herb seeds such as coriander, anise, fennel, sesame, and poppy

Blend first six ingredients and minced herb leaves (not seeds) to form dough. Roll between sheets of waxed paper into a 1-inch-thick rope and freeze on a cookie sheet.

Remove top sheet of paper and cut the frozen dough into 1-inch-long pieces. Place the dough, cut side up, on a baking sheet; or place into resealable freezer bags and freeze until baking day.

Bake at 325° for 5 minutes or until the edges are golden brown.

Alternatively, omit the herb leaves. After baking, sprinkle seeds on top of cookies, pressing them in while cookies are still hot.

rose geranium cake

12 medium-size rose geranium leaves, destemmed
2 sticks butter (plus bits of butter to prepare the pan)
2 cups sugar
2 cups flour
6 large eggs
powdered sugar for dusting

Have butter at room temperature. Do not preheat the oven. Wash and pat dry rose geranium leaves. Arrange them with their tops against the bottom and sides of a heavily buttered fluted cake pan. Use bits of butter to adhere rebellious leaves to the pan.

Beat butter and sugar until creamy. Add 2 eggs and beat until light and fluffy. Add 1 cup of flour and 2 eggs. Blend well and beat for 1 minute. Repeat with remaining flour and eggs. Beat the batter for 1 minute. Spoon it into the prepared pan. Place in a cold oven. Do not open the oven door during baking.

Bake for 1 hour at 350°. Test for doneness by inserting a toothpick into the center of the cake; if it comes out clean, the cake is done. Leaves will be tan, not brown. Cool cake in pan for 10 minutes on a rack; then invert pan onto another rack to finish cooling.

Dust the cake with powdered sugar. Decorate the serving plate by tucking scented geranium leaves around the edge of the cake. Serve slices of cake with whipped cream mixed with minced rose petals; or serve with ice cream or lemon thyme ice (see *page 103*).

mistake-proof herb cake

left: **Rose-scented geranium leaves add pretty counterpoints to the light, sweet consistency of a traditional fluted cake. Serve the cake for dessert or as the highlight of a tea party.**

lavender wands

zones	time	skill
3–10	weekend	moderate

you will need

10 to 15 sprigs of fresh, long-stemmed lavender

strong thread

scissors

ribbon

lovely lavender

One of the most fragrant and durably scented herbs, lavender belongs in every garden. Lavender adds texture, as well as fragrance and color to beds, borders, and walkways when you use its soft gray-green foliage as an edging. Use lavender as critter control around a vegetable garden, as the centerpiece of an herb garden, or set in containers as decoration. The foliage is almost as fragrant as the flowers, which come in pale and dark lavender, pink, and white.

Lavender adapts to many indoor uses. The flowers dry well on the stems. Strip the flowers off the stems and use them to make sweet-scented sachets; or turn the flowers into sachets known as lavender wands or lavender bottles. This pretty, traditional craft makes attractive drawer fresheners and lovely gifts.

Other fragrant herbs and heirloom roses retain their scents when dried and combine wonderfully with lavender in potpourris, sachets, and concoctions for the bath. Add to these botanicals the bright note of citrus-scented herbs, such as lemon balm or lemon verbena. Adding rosemary, mint, southernwood, ground orange peel, and ground clove to lavender makes a moth-chasing sachet for closets and dresser drawers.

traditional craft

right: **Making fragrant lavender wands requires little in the way of materials and tools. This charming Victorian craft also takes little time.**

1 form the wand Gather the fresh lavender stems into a bunch. Tie the stems with strong thread, wrapping it at the base of the flower heads and knotting the thread to secure it.

Working around the bunch in one direction, bend each stem of lavender back over the flowers to enclose them.

Once all the stems are bent back, arrange them as evenly as possible around the flowers. Tie the stems again with thread at the base of the flowers.

An alternative method entails bending the stems over the flower heads and then weaving ¼-inch ribbon over and under the stems until the flower heads are completely woven with ribbon.

2 finish Wrap ribbon around the wand to cover the thread; tie the ribbon into a bow. If desired, tie the bottom of the stems with thread to secure them.

Place your lavender wands in drawers, with stored clothes or stationery, and in linen closets to impart their summery scent throughout the year.

Give your friends bouquets of lavender wands as gifts.

herbal potpourri

zones	time	skill
3–10	2–3 hours	easy

you will need

- 3 tablespoons orris root
- 20 drops damask rose oil
- 10 drops lavender oil
- 4 cups dried rose petals (red, fragrant)
- 2 cups dried rose-scented geranium leaves
- 2 cups dried lavender flowers
- 1 cup dried rosemary leaves
- 1 cup dried lemon verbena leaves
- 3 tablespoons gum benzoin
- 2 tablespoons each ground allspice, ground cloves, and cinnamon pieces

super scents

Make potpourri with dried flowers, buds, and leaves. Use only crispy-dry plant material; moisture leads to mold. Store the materials separately in covered airtight containers so they retain their scents until you use them. Place the finished potpourri in decorative jars or bowls with or without lids. If you keep the potpourri covered when not in use, the fragrance will last longer.

As uncovered potpourri ages, it loses some of its scent. Refresh it by adding a few drops of one or more of the essential oils you originally used to make the potpourri.

Use essential oils sparingly. These pure, concentrated essences of herbs, flowers, spices, and resins are available at food co-ops and herb stores.

lasting impressions

right: **The compelling fragrances and the attractive dried flowers and foliage of potpourri add to a room's ambiance for months.**

1 easy mixing Combine orris root and essential oils in a glass or ceramic bowl (plastic and wood absorb scents). Add the dried flowers and herbs, gum benzoin (available at herb or crafts stores), and spices. Orris root and gum benzoin preserve the scents. Pour the mixture into an airtight glass jar; cover and set aside to cure for two weeks; shake the jar every few days.

2 improvise Vary the scent of your potpourri by blending different oils and dried materials. Make a summery potpourri, for example, by combining citrus oils, such as lemon, lime, mandarin, or tangerine, with the dried rind of oranges and lemons. Add the dried leaves of lemon-scented herbs, such as lemon verbena, lemon balm, lemon thyme, and scented geranium. Stir in handfuls of rose petals for bulk.

bay leaf sachets Keep moths out of pantries and linen closets with adorable sachets. With the right sides of muslin or printed fabric together, cut simple shapes, such as bunnies or hearts, cutting two pieces for each sachet. Sew pieces together, leaving a ¼-inch seam allowance and a 1-inch opening. Turn the fabric right side out through the opening. Fill with crushed herbs and spices, such as bay combined with lavender and clove, rose petals and cinnamon, or lemon balm and allspice. Use batting or rice to give the sachets body. Hand-stitch the opening of the sachet closed.

herbal cosmetics

zones	time	skill
3–10	10 minutes	easy

you will need

- 2 cups mineral water
- $^1/_4$ cup vodka
- 8 drops lavender essential oil
- glass bottles with stoppers

fragrant waters

Making scented water to use as a body splash or facial mist couldn't be easier. Mix the ingredients in a glass measuring cup; then pour the blend into clean bottles. The recipe makes 2 cups. Refrigerate and use within a week. If desired, substitute rose essential oil for the lavender.

Or make herbal infusions for a bath or a facial splash. Pour 4 cups of boiling water over 4 tablespoons of fresh herbs; cover and steep for 10 minutes. Strain and use.

summer coolers

right: **Rose and lavender waters make soothing facial splashes for hot summer days.**

tootsy bath

left: Enjoy your own at-home spa treatments. Soak tired feet in a foot bath made with warm water, a few drops of liquid soap, fresh rosemary, and marbles. Massage your feet on the marbles while the warm water releases the soothing scent of the rosemary. As another option, treat your face to an invigorating cleansing by adding a handful of rosemary or lavender to a pan of boiling water. Turn off the stove. Tent a towel over your head and the pan of steaming water, holding your face about a foot above the water for five minutes.

herbal essences

left: Harvest the potent essences of your favorite herbs and flowers by capturing them the old-fashioned way—in bottles. Pick plant materials at their peak, in the early morning, and place them in glass containers large enough to keep the material from touching the bottom of the glass. Seal tightly and set the jars in the sun for three days. Strain the fluids that collect at the bottom of the bottles. Use the liquid within a day or two by dabbing it on your face.

the
plants

common and botanical names

aloe
Aloe vera

angelica
Angelica archangelica

artemisia
Artemisia species

basil
Ocimum basilicum

bay
Laurus nobilis

bee balm (bergamot)
Monarda didyma

borage
Borago officinalis

calamint
Calamintha species

calendula (pot marigold)
Calendula officinalis

caraway
Carum carvi

catnip
Nepeta cataria

cayenne
Capsicum annuum var. annuum

chamomile
Chamaemelum nobile

chervil
Anthriscus cerefolium

chives/garlic/garlic chives
Allium species

comfrey
Symphytum officinale

cilantro (coriander)
Coriandrum sativum

dill
Anethum graveolens

elder (elderberry)
Sambucus canadensis

fennel
Foeniculum vulgare

feverfew
Tanacetum parthenium

florentine iris (orris root)
Iris germanica var. florentina

germander
Teucrium species

ginger
Zingiber officinale

goldenseal
Hydrastis canadensis

hops
Humulus lupulus

horehound
Marrubium vulgare

horseradish
Armoracia rusticana

horsetail
Equisetum hyemale

hyssop
Hyssop officinalis

lady's mantle
Alchemilla mollis

lavender
Lavandula species and hybrids

lemon balm
Melissa officinalis

lemongrass
Cymbopogon citratus

lemon verbena
Aloysia triphylla

lovage
Levisticum officinale

elderberry

marsh mallow
  Althaea officinalis

mint
  Mentha species

oregano
  Origanum vulgare

parsley
  Petroselinum crispum

purple coneflower
  Echinacea species

rosemary
  Rosmarinus species and hybrids

rue
  Ruta graveolens

sage
  Salvia officinalis

salad burnet (garden burnet)
  Sanguisorba minor

sorrel
  Rumex species

st. john's wort
  Hypericum species

stevia (sugar leaf)
  Stevia serrata

sweet cicely
  Myrrhis odorata

sweet marjoram
  Origanum majorana

sweet woodruff
  Galium odoratum

tarragon (french tarragon)
  Artemisia dracunculus

thyme
  Thymus species

valerian
  Valeriana officinalis

willow
  Salix species

winter savory
  Satureja montana

garlic chives

the plants

Alchemilla mollis

lady's mantle

Perennial with chartreuse flowers in summer.
Light: full sun or light shade
Size: 8–10 inches tall
Zones: 3–8
Lovely edging a border or patio. Use flowers in
arrangements; leaves in tea and cosmetics.
Preserve by air drying. Propagate by division
or seeds.

Allium species

chives/garlic/garlic chives

Perennials with pale purple or white flowers in
late spring.
Light: full sun
Size: 10–12 inches tall
Zones: 5–9
Pretty edging a garden or in a container. Use
flowers, fresh or dried, in arrangements;
leaves or bulbs in cooking. Garlic is known for
lowering blood pressure. Preserve chives by
freezing minced leaves; air-dry flowers.
Propagate by division, cloves, or seeds.

Aloe vera

aloe

Succulent that grows easily indoors.
Light: full sun
Size: 1–2 feet tall
Zones: 8–11
Sap from the leaves soothes cuts and burns.
Grows well on an indoor windowsill; prefers
dry soil. Propagate by offsets or division.

Aloysia triphylla

lemon verbena

Deciduous shrub with white or lilac flowers
in summer.
Light: full sun
Size: 3–6 feet tall
Zones: 8–11
Use leaves, which have an intense lemon
flavor, in teas or cooking (remove before
serving). In colder zones grow in a pot and
bring plant indoors in winter. Preserve by
air-drying. Propagate by stem cuttings;
air-layering.

lady's mantle

chives

aloe

lemon verbena

marsh mallow

dill

angelica

chervil

Althaea officinalis
marsh mallow
Perennial with light pink flowers from midsummer to fall.
Light: full sun
Size: 2–5 feet tall
Zones: 3–8
Pretty in cutting or herb gardens; prefers moist soil. In ancient times, tea made from its dried roots and leaves was used to soothe sore throats. Cut flowers for arrangements. Propagate by division or seeds.

Anethum graveolens
dill
Annual with yellow flowers in summer.
Light: full sun
Size: 2–4 feet tall
Zones: all
Good background plant; use dwarf varieties in containers. Sow two to three times during the season. Use flowers and seeds in pickling; use leaves, fresh or dried, in cooking and salads. Preserve by air-drying. Propagate by seeds.

Angelica archangelica
angelica
Biennial with greenish white or cream flowers in summer.
Light: light shade
Size: 4–6 feet tall
Zones: 4–8
Prefers moist soil; self-sows readily. Stems, leaves, and roots taste like licorice. Use in baking or in flavoring liqueurs. Preserve stems by freezing. Propagate by seeds.

Anthriscus cerefolium
chervil
Annual with white flowers in summer.
Light: light shade
Size: 1–2 feet tall
Zones: all
Plant in spring and fall. Cut off flower buds to keep plants producing leaves, which have a mild anise flavor. Use in salads, vegetables, or eggs. Preserve by freezing minced leaves blended with water. Propagate by seeds.

the plants

Armoracia rusticana
horseradish
Perennial with white flowers in late spring.
Light: full or partial sun
Size: 1½–2 feet tall
Zones: 5–8
Spreads rapidly, almost uncontrollably. Plant in an out-of-the-way spot or in a container. Harvest roots after frost. Peel, chop in a blender, store in refrigerator, and use to season many dishes. Propagates itself.

Artemisia species
artemisia
Perennial and annual with flowers in summer; many have silvery leaves.
Light: full sun
Size: 1–3 feet tall
Zones: 4–9
Ornamental and fragrant, varieties include 'Sweet Annie', 'Silver King', 'Powis Castle', mugwort, wormwood, and southernwood. Use flowers and foliage in arrangements and wreaths. Preserve by air-drying. Propagate by division or stem cuttings.

Artemisia dracunculus
tarragon (french tarragon)
Perennial.
Light: full sun or light shade
Size: 2–3 feet tall
Zones: 3–8
Sweet, anise flavor. Use in vinegars and with chicken, fish, and vegetables. Preserve by air-drying. Propagate only by division or root cuttings, not seeds.

Borago officinalis
borage
Annual with blue flowers in summer.
Light: full sun
Size: 1½–2 feet tall
Zones: all
Pink buds open to blue flowers. Use the cucumber-flavor stems, leaves, and flowers in salads, teas, fruit, or wine drinks. Propagate by seeds; self-sows.

horseradish

tarragon

artemisia

borage

calamint

calendula

cayenne

caraway

Calamintha species

calamint

Perennial with mauve, pink, red, or white flowers from summer to fall.

Light: full sun or light shade

Size: 1-2 feet tall

Zones: 5–9

Lovely edging a border or path. Use the mint-scented gray-green leaves in teas and cooking. Preserve by air-drying. Propagate by seeds.

Calendula officinalis

calendula (pot marigold)

Annual with orange, apricot, yellow, or cream flowers in summer to fall.

Light: full sun

Size: 1½-2 feet tall

Zones: all

The ancient application of a tincture of the flowers as an external anti-inflammatory is still in use. Grow in pots indoors for winter. Use flowers for arrangements; minced, fresh or dried, they give the same color as saffron to rice. Propagate by seeds.

Capsicum annuum var. *annuum*

cayenne

Annual with bright red fruit in summer.

Light: full sun

Size: 1½-2 feet tall

Zones: 4–10

Great for color in the garden or in pots; hot flavor in dishes. Use ripe red fruit; wear gloves when preparing them. Preserve by grinding air-dried peppers. Propagate by seeds started indoors.

Carum carvi

caraway

Biennial with white flowers followed by seeds the second year.

Light: full sun

Size: 1½-2 feet tall

Zones: 3–9

Very pretty in the garden. Use young leaves to flavor soups and salads; use flowers in arrangements. Preserve seeds by air-drying thoroughly: Hang seed heads upside down in a paper bag and check for insects before storing in jars. Propagate by seeds; self-sows.

the plants

Chamaemelum nobile
chamomile

Perennial with daisylike flowers in summer.
Light: full sun or light shade
Size: 5–6 inches tall
Zones: 4–8
Tolerates light foot traffic; plant between stepping-stones or in an herbal lawn. Dried flowers make a soothing tea. Do not drink if you are allergic to ragweed or other members of the *Compositae* (daisy) family. Preserve by air-drying. Propagate by seeds or division.

Coriandrum sativum
cilantro (coriander)

Annual with white flowers in early summer.
Light: full sun
Size: 2–2½ feet tall
Zones: all
Sow every two to three weeks from spring to fall; plants go to seed quickly in hot weather. Use fresh leaves (cilantro) or crushed seeds (coriander) in cooking. Also grows well in a pot indoors. Propagate by seeds.

Cymbopogon citratus
lemongrass

Tender perennial with greenish white flowers in late summer.
Light: full sun
Size: 3–6 feet tall
Zones: 9–11
Ornamental with distinct lemon flavor. Grow in a container and bring indoors for winter. Use fresh or dried leaves in cooking (Thai, in particular) and teas. Preserve by air-drying. Propagate by division.

Echinacea species
purple coneflower

Perennial with pale purple flowers in summer.
Light: full sun
Size: 3–4 feet tall
Zones: 3–8
Ornamental. Seed heads attract birds to the garden. Used medicinally to enhance the immune system. Preserve by air-drying. Propagate by division or seeds.

chamomile

cilantro/coriander

lemongrass

purple coneflower

horsetail

fennel

sweet woodruff

hops

Equisetum hyemale

horsetail

Perennial with unbranched stems that remain green over winter.

Light: full sun or light shade

Size: 2–3 feet tall

Zones: 3–8

Good accent in moist soil near a pond. Plant in containers; it spreads invasively by underground roots. Brushy growth has been used for centuries to scour pots. Preserve by air-drying. Propagate by root division.

Foeniculum vulgare

fennel

Perennial with yellow flowers in summer.

Light: full sun

Size: 4–6 feet tall

Zones: 4–10

Resembles dill, which it cross-pollinates readily, resulting in plants with little flavor. Foliage and flowers have an anise scent and flavor. Plant the bronze-leaf variety. Use fresh leaves or flowers in salads, butters, vegetables, and with fish; use crushed seeds in baking. Propagate by seeds; self-sows.

Galium odoratum

sweet woodruff

Perennial with white flowers in late spring.

Light: light to deep shade

Size: 6–10 inches tall

Zones: 4–8

Pretty groundcover for the edge of a woodland. The dried foliage smells like vanilla or fresh-cut hay. Make traditional May wine by pouring white wine into a jar stuffed with fresh leaves. The herb contains coumarin. Propagate by division.

Humulus lupulus

hops

Perennial vine with female cone-shape flowers in late summer.

Light: full sun or light shade

Size: 10–20 feet tall

Zones: 5–8

Plants cover arbors quickly. Use the flowers (actually fruits of female plants) in brewing beer. Dry flowers. Propagate by division, seeds, or stem cuttings.

the plants

Hydrastis canadensis

goldenseal

Perennial with greenish white flowers in late spring, decorative red berries in summer.

Light: light shade

Size: 1–1½ feet tall

Zones: 3–8

Wild plants are endangered in several states due to overharvesting the roots, which are thought to have antibacterial and antiviral qualities in soothing teas and ointments. Preserve by air-drying. Propagate by division or seeds.

Hypericum species

st. john's wort

Shrubs and perennials with yellow flowers in mid- to late summer.

Light: full sun or light shade

Size: 2–3 feet tall

Zones: 6–9

Beautiful in the garden. The leaves and flowers are used as a treatment for mild depression. Use flowers and foliage in teas. Preserve by air-drying. Propagate by division or seeds.

Hyssop officinalis

hyssop

Perennial with blue flowers in late summer.

Light: full sun or light shade

Size: 1½–3 feet tall

Zones: 3–8

Pretty in a border or as a low hedge; it attracts bees. Use dried flowers and leaves in potpourris, leaves in soothing teas. Preserve by air-drying. Propagate by division, seeds, or stem cuttings.

Iris germanica var. *florentina*

florentine iris (orris root)

Perennial with white flowers in late spring.

Light: full sun or light shade

Size: 2–3 feet tall

Zones: 5–8

Roots are a source of orris root (a fragrant preservative); scrape, air-dry, and chop for use in potpourris. Propagate by division or seeds.

goldenseal

st. john's wort

florentine iris

hyssop

Laurus nobilis

bay

Evergreen tree.
Light: full sun
Size: 8 or more feet tall
Zones: 8–10
Attractive in a container; grow indoors year-round or overwinter in cold zones. Use whole leaves in culinary dishes, such as stews and soups. Preserve by air-drying. Propagate by cuttings or seeds (both methods are slow).

Lavandula species

lavender

Shrub with lavender, purple, pink, or white flowers in early summer.
Light: full sun
Size: 1–2 feet tall
Zones: 5–9, depending on species
Lovely edging a border, an herb garden, a patio, or in containers. Use flowers and foliage in arrangements, potpourris, cooking, and beauty treatments. Preserve by air-drying. Propagate by division or seeds.

Levisticum officinale

lovage

Perennial with greenish yellow flowers in early summer.
Light: full sun or light shade
Size: 4–6 feet tall
Zones: 3–8
Enticing background plant. Flavor similar to celery. Use leaves in salads and soups; ground seeds in cakes and breads. Preserve by air-drying. Propagate by division or seeds.

Marrubium vulgare

horehound

Perennial with white flowers in summer.
Light: full sun
Size: 1–2 feet tall
Zones: 4–8
A member of the mint family, it spreads rapidly and is widely considered a weed. Use leaves (fresh for best flavor) in teas to soothe sore throats and colds. Propagate by division or seeds.

the plants

Melissa officinalis
lemon balm
Perennial with white flowers in summer.
Light: full sun or very light shade
Size: 2–2½ feet tall
Zones: 4–8
Lemon scent and flavor. A mint family member that is invasive. Use leaves in arrangements, teas, and sachets. Preserve by air-drying. Propagate by division or seeds; self-sows readily.

Mentha species
mint
Perennial with white to purple flowers in mid- to late summer.
Light: full sun or light shade
Size: 2–3 feet tall
Zones: 4–8
Many varieties, from orange and apple to spearmint and peppermint; all grow rampantly. Use flowers in arrangements; use leaves in teas, salads, and vegetables. Preserve by air-drying or freezing. Propagate by division.

Monarda didyma
bee balm (bergamot)
Perennial with red, pink, white, or violet flowers in summer.
Light: light shade
Size: 3–5 feet tall
Zones: 3–8
A favorite of bees and hummingbirds. Leaves have a citrus fragrance and flavor. Use fresh flowers ornamentally; fresh or dried leaves in tea, salads, and potpourris. Preserve by air-drying. Propagate by division or stem cuttings.

Myrrhis odorata
sweet cicely
Perennial with white flowers in spring.
Light: light shade or shade
Size: 2–2½ feet tall
Zones: 3–7
All parts are edible. Use fresh anise-scented leaves in salads, leaves in tea, seeds in pastries, and peeled root in stir-fries. Preserve seeds by air-drying. Propagate by root division or seeds; self-sows readily.

lemon balm

mint

bee balm

sweet cicely

catnip

basil

sweet marjoram

oregano

Nepeta cataria
catnip
Perennial with white, blue-spotted flowers in midsummer.
Light: full sun or light shade
Size: 2–3 feet tall
Zones: 3–8
A feline favorite. Use fresh or dried leaves in a soothing tea; use dried leaves for cat treats. Preserve by air-drying. Propagate by division, stem cuttings, layering, or seeds; self-sows.

Ocimum basilicum
basil
Annual with white or rosy pink flowers in summer.
Light: full sun
Size: 1-2 feet tall
Zones: all
Grows well in containers, indoors or out. Many varieties, from lemon- and spicy-scented to purple-leaf, lettuce-leaf, and dwarf forms. Use leaves in pestos, vinegars, salads, and sauces. Preserve by freezing or air-drying. Propagate by seeds.

Origanum majorana
sweet marjoram
Tender perennial with white or pale violet flowers in late summer.
Light: full sun
Size: 1½–2 feet tall
Zones: 8–10
Grow in a pot to bring indoors over winter. Flavor more delicate than oregano. Use flowers and leaves in egg dishes, vegetables, and pasta. Preserve by air-drying. Propagate by seeds or root cuttings.

Origanum vulgare
oregano
Perennial with purple or white flowers in midsummer.
Light: full sun
Size: 1–2½ feet tall
Zones: 6–9
Pungent flavor. Use in Italian and Greek dishes, soups, stews, tomato sauces, and meat dishes. Preserve by air-drying. Propagate by division or seeds.

the plants

Petroselinum crispum
parsley
Biennial treated as annual.
Light: full sun or light shade
Size: 8–12 inches tall
Zones: 6–9
Both curly- and flat-leaf parsley grow well indoors. High in vitamin C. Use leaves fresh for best flavor in almost any dish. Preserve by drying or freezing. Propagate by seeds, which take from two to three weeks to germinate.

Rosmarinus species and hybrids
rosemary
Tender perennial with blue or white flowers in late spring or early summer.
Light: full sun
Size: 6 inches to 5 feet tall
Zones: 8–10
Beautiful in the garden or in containers. Bring indoors over winter in colder zones. Prostrate, dwarf form makes an excellent groundcover. Use the pine-scented leaves in cooking and potpourris. Preserve by air-drying. Propagate by stem cuttings.

Rumex species
sorrel/french sorrel
Perennials that grow poorly in hot weather; flowers in summer.
Light: full sun or light shade
Size: 1½–2 feet tall
Zones: 4–8
Cut back before flowering to increase new leaf production. Leaves add flavor to salads and soups. Best used fresh, but preserve by freezing. Propagate by division or seeds.

Ruta graveolens
rue
Perennial with yellow flowers in midsummer.
Light: full sun
Size: 2–3 feet tall
Zones: 4–8
Lovely ornamental planted to repel pests. Foliage may cause skin rash. Use fresh foliage and dried seedpods in arrangements. Propagate by division, cuttings, or seeds.

parsley

sorrel

rosemary

rue

willow

sage

elder

salad burnet

Salix species
willow
Tree and shrub forms with green, yellow, or
black bark.
Light: full sun
Size: 5–20 feet tall
Zones: 3–8
Various ornamental species that thrive in moist
soil. Original source of substance used for
making aspirin. Stems used in basketmaking.

Salvia officinalis
sage
Perennial with purple flowers in late spring.
Light: full sun or light shade
Size: 2–3 feet tall
Zones: 5–8
Textured gray-green foliage. Variegated forms,
such as 'Tricolor' and golden sage, have milder
flavors. Cut back woody stems by two-thirds
in spring to encourage new growth. Use
flowers in arrangements; use leaves in teas and
cooking. Preserve by air-drying. Propagate by
division, stem cuttings, or seeds.

Sambucus canadensis
elder (elderberry)
Deciduous shrub with ivory flowers in early
summer and large clusters of berries.
Light: full sun or light shade
Size: 10–15 feet tall
Zones: 4–7
Pretty in a natural setting, where birds devour
the berries. Use flowers in teas and cooling
drinks; berries in making elderberry wine, pie,
and jam. Propagate by cuttings or seeds.

Sanguisorba minor
salad burnet (garden burnet)
Perennial with rose flowers in late summer.
Light: full sun
Size: 1–2 feet tall (with flower stalks)
Zones: 4–8
Attractive edging along a border. Use young
leaves, which taste like cucumber, in iced
drinks, salads, and vinegars; flowers are also
edible. Preserve leaves in vinegar; they do not
dry well. Propagate by division or seeds.

the plants

Satureja species

savory

Perennials with flowering tips in late summer.
Light: full sun
Size: 1- 1½ feet tall
Zones: 5–8
Harvest frequently to keep plants compact. Use in vinegars and poultry seasoning. Preserve by air-drying. Propagate by division, cuttings, or seeds.

Stevia serrata

stevia (sugar leaf)

Tender perennial or annual with white or pink flowers in summer.
Light: full sun or light shade
Size: 1½–3 feet tall
Zones: 8–11
The leaves are 20 to 30 times sweeter than sugar and are nearly calorie-free. Use fresh or dried leaves as a sugar substitute in teas and baking. Preserve by air-drying. Propagate by division or seeds.

Symphytum officinale

comfrey

Perennial with pink, violet, or white flowers in late spring to midsummer.
Light: full sun or light shade
Size: 2½–3 feet tall
Zones: 3–8
Good for herb gardens, borders, woodland edges, and meadow plantings. For centuries leaves and roots have been used externally to heal wounds. Propagate by division, cuttings, or seeds.

Tanacetum parthenium

feverfew

Perennial with white flowers in late spring.
Light: full sun or very light shade
Size: 1–3 feet tall
Zones: 5–8
Good in mixed plantings. Tansy (*Tanacetum vulgare*) is a cousin with yellow flowers. Reblooms if cut back after first flowering. Use flowers in arrangements; strew leaves to repel insects. Propagate by division or seeds; self-sows.

savory

stevia

comfrey

feverfew

germander

valerian

thyme

ginger

Teucrium species
germander
Woody perennial with pinkish purple flowers in late summer.
Light: full sun or very light shade
Size: 1½–2 feet tall
Zones: 5–8
Use upright, glossy-leaf varieties as hedge plants for knot gardens or edging. Cut back in spring and after flowering to maintain a green border. Propagate by division or seeds.

Thymus species
thyme
Perennial with pink or white flowers in spring.
Light: full sun
Size: 3–12 inches tall
Zones: 4–8
Versatile plant for any garden and containers. Try silver- and golden-edge, as well as lemon-scented varieties. Use sprigs in soups, stews, and vegetable dishes; lemon-scented leaves in potpourris and teas. Preserve by air-drying. Propagate by division, layering, or seeds.

Valeriana officinalis
valerian
Perennial with white flowers in early summer.
Light: full sun or light shade
Size: 4–5 feet tall
Zones: 4–8
Decorative at the back of a garden. Dried rhizomes (roots) are used to make extract that treats anxiety and insomnia. Propagate by division or seeds.

Zingiber officinale
ginger
Tender perennial with yellow or white flowers in summer.
Light: full sun or light shade
Size: 3–5 feet tall
Zones: 10–11
Grow in a deep pot; bring indoors for winter. Peel and chop roots for use in Asian dishes, curries, and baking. Preserve by slicing and air-drying; grind to a powder. Used to treat motion sickness and indigestion. Propagate by root division; start with those that you buy at the store.

sources

mail-order nurseries and garden suppliers

Burpee (H, P, S) free
300 Park Ave.
Warminster, PA 18991-0001
800/333-5808
www.burpee.com

The Cook's Garden (S) free
P.O. Box 535
Londonderry, VT 05148
800/457-9703
www.cooksgarden.com

Dabney's Herbs (P) $2.00
P.O. Box 22061
Louisville, KY 40252
502/893-5198
www.dabneyherbs.com

Forestfarm (H, P) free
990 Tetherow Rd.
Williams, OR 97544-9599
541/846-7269
www.forestfarm.com

Gardener's Supply Co. (H) free
128 Intervale Rd.
Burlington, VT 05401
888/833-1412
www.gardeners.com

Kinsman Co. (H) free
P.O. Box 428
Point Pleasant, PA 18950-0357
800/733-4146
www.kinsmangarden.com

Logee's Greenhouses (P) $4.95
141 North St.
Danielson, CT 06239-1939
888/330-8038
www.logees.com

Long Creek Herbs (H, P) free
P.O. Box 127
Blue Eye, MO 65611
417/779-5450
www.longcreekherbs.com

Papa Geno's Herb Farm (H, P, S) free
11125 S. 14th St.
St. Roca, NE 68430
402/423-5051
www.papagenos.com

Martha's Herbary (H, P) free
589 Pomfret St.
P.O. Box 236
Pomfret, CT 06258
860/928-0009
www.marthasherbary.com

Nichol's Garden Nursery (P) free
1190 Old Salem Rd. NE
Albany, OR 97321-4580
541/928-9280
800/231-5306 fax
www.nicholsgardennursery.com

Park Seed (H, P, S) free
1 Parkton Ave.
Greenwood, SC 29649
800/213-0076
www.parkseed.com

Peaceful Valley Farm Supply (H) free
P.O. Box 2209
Grass Valley, CA 95945
888/784-1722
www.groworganic.com

Pinetree Garden Seeds (S) free
Box 300
New Gloucester, ME 04260
207/926-3400
www.superseeds.com

Raintree Nursery (H, P) free
391 Butts Rd.
Morton, WA 98356
360/496-6400
888/770-8358 fax
www.raintreenursery.com

Renee's Garden (S) free
7389 W. Zayante Rd.
Felton, CA 95018
888/880-7228
www.reneesgarden.com

Richters Herbs (S) free
357 Highway 47
Goodwood, Ontario
Canada L0C1A0
905/640-6677
www.richters.com

Sandy Mush Herb Nursery (P) free
316 Surrett Cove Rd.
Leicester, NC 28748-5517
828/683-2014
www.brwm.org/sandymushherbs

usda plant hardiness zone maps

These maps of climate zones can help you select plants for your garden that will survive a typical winter in your region. The United States Department of Agriculture (USDA) developed them, basing the zones on the lowest recorded temperatures across the country. On a scale of 1 to 11, Zone 1 is the coldest area and Zone 11 is the warmest.

Plants are classified by the coldest temperature and zone they can endure. For example, plants hardy to Zone 6 survive where winter temperatures drop to –10° F. Those hardy to Zone 8 die long before it's that cold. These plants may grow in colder regions but must be replaced each year. Plants rated for a range of Hardiness Zones can usually survive winter in the coldest region, as well as tolerate the summer heat of the warmest one.

To find your Hardiness Zone, note the approximate location of your community on the map; then match the color band marking that area to the key.

Hawaii

Australia

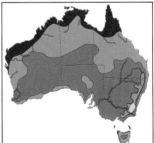

United Kingdom

Range of Average Annual Minimum Temperatures for Each Zone

Zone 1: Below -50° F (below -45.6° C)
Zone 2: -50 to -40° F (-45.5 to -40° C)
Zone 3: -40 to -30° F (-39.9 to -34.5° C)
Zone 4: -30 to -20° F (-34.4 to -28.9° C)
Zone 5: -20 to -10° F (-28.8 to -23.4° C)
Zone 6: -10 to 0° F (-23.3 to -17.8° C)
Zone 7: 0 to 10° F (-17.7 to -12.3° C)
Zone 8: 10 to 20° F (-12.2 to -6.7° C)
Zone 9: 20 to 30° F (-6.6 to -1.2° C)
Zone 10: 30 to 40° F (-1.1 to 4.4° C)
Zone 11: Above 40° F (above 4.5° C)

index

index

index

photo credits

metric conversions

us units to metric equivalents			metric units to us equivalents		
to convert from	multiply by	to get	to convert from	multiply by	to get
Inches	25.400	Millimeters	Millimeters	0.0394	Inches
Inches	2.540	Centimeters	Centimeters	0.3937	Inches
Feet	30.480	Centimeters	Centimeters	0.0328	Feet
Feet	0.3048	Meters	Meters	3.2808	Feet
Yards	0.9144	Meters	Meters	1.0936	Yards
Square inches	6.4516	Square centimeters	Square centimeters	0.1550	Square inches
Square feet	0.0929	Square meters	Square meters	10.764	Square feet
Square yards	0.8361	Square meters	Square meters	1.1960	Square yards
Acres	0.4047	Hectares	Hectares	2.4711	Acres
Cubic inches	16.387	Cubic centimeters	Cubic centimeters	0.0610	Cubic inches
Cubic feet	0.0283	Cubic meters	Cubic meters	35.315	Cubic feet
Cubic feet	28.316	Liters	Liters	0.0353	Cubic feet
Cubic yards	0.7646	Cubic meters	Cubic meters	1.308	Cubic yards
Cubic yards	764.550	Liters	Liters	0.0013	Cubic yards

To convert from degrees Celsius (C) to degrees Fahrenheit (F), multiply by ⁹⁄₅, then add 32.

To convert from degrees Fahrenheit (F) to degrees Celsius (C), first subtract 32, then multiply by ⁵⁄₉.